EUCLID

THE FATHER OF GEOMETRY

THE **GREATEST** GREEK PHILOSOPHERS

EUCLID

THE FATHER OF GEOMETRY

JOSETTE CAMPBELL & CHRIS HAYHURST

ROSEN PUBLISHING
NEW YORK

Published in 2016 by The Rosen Publishing Group, Inc.
29 East 21st Street, New York, NY 10010

First Edition

Library of Congress Cataloging-in-Publication Data

Campbell, Josette, author.
Euclid: the father of geometry/Josette Campbell and Chris Hayhurst.—First edition.
pages cm.—(The greatest Greek philosophers)
Includes bibliographical references and index.
ISBN 978-1-4994-6128-2 (library bound)
1. Euclid—Juvenile literature. 2. Mathematicians—Greece—Biography—Juvenile literature. 3. Mathematics, Greek—Juvenile literature. 4. Geometry—History—Juvenile literature. I. Hayhurst, Chris, author. II. Title.
QA29.E78C36 2016
510.92—dc23
[B]

2014048139

Manufactured in the United States of America

Contents

Euclidean geometry is the foundation of the geometry classes that are taught in high school. It is the study of flat planes, straight lines, points, and solid figures. The word "geometry" comes from the Greek *ge* ("earth") and *metria* ("a measuring of"), and means earth measuring. Euclidean geometry is based on the axioms and theorems of the Greek mathematician Euclid, who lived in the third century BCE. This resource offers a look into Euclid's life and contributions to mathematics, as much as can be gleaned from the historical records and commentaries that survive today.

The world two thousand years ago was a very different place from what it is today. The Internet and Wi-Fi did not exist. There were no laptops, tablets, HD TVs, MP3 players, cell phones, video games, digital cameras, or electronics of any kind. Automobiles, nuclear submarines, and jet airplanes did not exist. Neither did dirt bikes, skateboards, or jet skis.

The world was much smaller then, although not in a literal sense. Earth was the same size it is today, and it traveled the same elliptical orbit around the sun. The world was much smaller in the sense that the people who lived on it knew very little about it. What they did know about was usually only the land on which they lived. Perhaps they had vague notions of other lands far away, much farther than they would ever dream of traveling. Daily life, for most people, followed the same

UCTION

routine. It was waking in the morning, working by day, and sleeping by night.

For some, however, including those who found themselves tucked away in the lush and prosperous lands that surrounded the Mediterranean Sea, the world of more than two thousand years ago was also a time of intense intellectual investigation. People asked questions and wondered about life. They also pondered existence and whether it held any meaning beyond what they could see before them. They were thinkers and dreamers, inventors and creators. They discovered an importance to life that those before them had never considered. They began to see the world as a place for unearthing answers to life's many mysteries.

Forget, if just for a while, the things that surround you, and instead immerse yourself in a world where life itself was a mystery. Step out of your chair and into the blue and green of the ancient Mediterranean Sea. Wade into the waters, as far as you dare. Set your imagination free. Then, if you can, turn around and look back toward the shore.

Welcome to ancient Greece. It is 300 BCE, more than 2,315 years ago. Before you, in a stone-walled courtyard encircled by olive trees, stands an assortment of people like you've never seen before. All of them are men. They stand in clusters, talking among themselves in loud, boisterous bursts of excitement and laughter.

This sculptural relief, influenced by Greek art, depicts a banquet scene from the early 300s BCE *in Alexandria, Egypt.*

They hold wine in what look like large, heavy earthen mugs. They drink the wine like water and eat ferociously from enormous tables made of thick, dark wood. Many of the men have long, gray beards. All have dense manes of scraggly hair. They stand barefoot or in sandals. Their clothes are light and robelike, just right for the warm winds that blow in from the nearby sea.

The men's voices grow louder as the sun begins to set. Servants move among the partygoers, replenishing the food as quickly as it is consumed. Finally, as the darkness sets in, one man pulls himself up onto a table and stands well above the others. A flaming torch just a few feet behind him sends his shadow dancing and leaping across the courtyard. The man raises his drink high above his head and, with dark, thoughtful eyes, looks out over his peers. The crowd grows silent. The man toasts someone named Euclid. And with that, the people, who have now all turned to face one man standing alone near the center of the courtyard, raise their drinks in the toast.

But wait a moment; take a step back. Who exactly is this man Euclid, or Euclid of Alexandria, sometimes Euclides of Alexandria, as some have called him? Why is he, of all people, the luminary of the evening? What did he do to deserve such a celebration?

Euclid was a mysterious man, almost more a legend than a real-life, flesh-and-blood historical figure. He did live in ancient Greece. That much historians know for sure. He did leave his mark on the world, mainly through one tremendously important book that he wrote. But beyond that, the rest is almost entirely speculation. There are no firsthand accounts of Euclid's physical appearance or portraits or any other depictions of him that have survived the ancient past. Historians specializing in ancient Greece have dug through countless reams of artifacts, searching for clues to the particulars of Euclid's life; however, nothing has been found.

Nevertheless, some things are known. Euclid, a mathematician, was born during Greece's Classical Age. This was a time, generally considered to be between around 480 BCE and 323 BCE, of unprecedented scientific, political, and philosophical progress and innovation. Many brilliant people lived during this time, producing works that would change the world. They weren't afraid to ask questions that had never been asked before, and they never hesitated to break new intellectual ground.

In Euclid's case this new ground was clear: it was the subject of mathematics, specifically geometry. Euclid took geometry to an entirely new level. It was he, perhaps more than anyone before him or after him, who shaped the subject into what it is today. As a result, he became known as the father of geometry. *Elements*, Euclid's thirteen-volume treatise on mathematics and geometry, was considered to be one of the most influential compilations in history. It inspired with its logical arrangement not only mathematicians and scientists but also politicians, including Abraham Lincoln.

Before delving deeper into the preeminent mathematician's life, however, one must first look at the lives and times of those who came before him. Euclid, after all, was a product of his times, the result of the centuries of thought and progress that came before him. It was the great English mathematician and physicist Sir Isaac Newton (1642–1727) who gave credit to his own predecessors with the following exclamation: "If I have seen further, it is by standing upon the shoulders of giants." Euclid, had he been alive during Newton's time to read those words, would have almost certainly agreed. Euclid, too, stood on the shoulders of giants. He, like Newton, saw farther than those who preceded him.

CHAPTER ONE

ANCIENT GREEK CIVILIZATION

On whatever occasion people discuss Euclid, who is generally believed to have flourished around 300 BCE (his birth and death dates are unknown), they cannot do so without referring to ancient Greek civilization.

Many historians acknowledge that Greek culture began with the demise of the Mycenaean civilization around 1200 BCE and ended with the death of Alexander the Great in 323 BCE. It was also the era of the Greek Classical Age, the period just before the beginning of the Persian Wars (492–449 BCE) and just after the death of Alexander the Great. It was a period of great achievement in the areas of politics, philosophy, art and architecture, literature, and science, including mathematics.

Much of what people feel deep affection for and appreciate about society today can be traced all the way back to the ancient Greeks. Democracy, for example, is the foundation of a free society in much of the world today. Without democracy, individuals wouldn't be allowed to vote for their leaders, stand up for their beliefs, or speak out against those with whom they disagree. Democracy allows people to play an active role in government and the management and day-to-day affairs of their nation. Democracy grants people the freedom to live the way they choose.

Democracy owes its birth to ancient Greece, especially to the most prominent Greek city of that time, Athens. Back then, "democracy" was known by the Greek

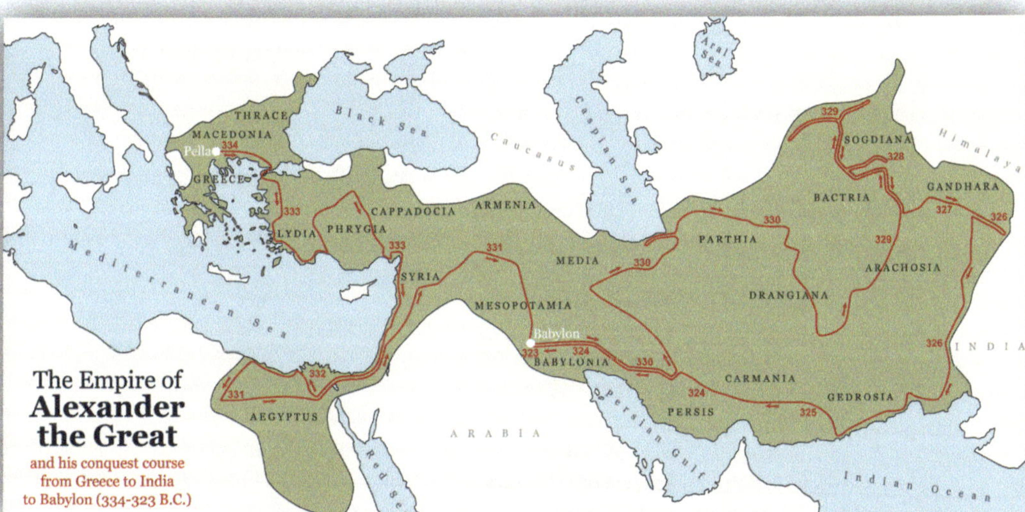

The empire of Alexander the Great extended from Greece east to India and south to Egypt. Many historians mark the end of ancient Greek civilization with the death of Alexander the Great in 323 BCE.

word *demokratia*, for "rule of the people." It was such an important concept to the Greeks that they even had a goddess, Demokratia, named after it.

THE POLIS ATHENS

Athens, a bustling polis, or city-state, near the end of a long finger of land jutting out toward the Mediterranean Sea, was the cultural center of the Greek-speaking world. People came to Athens from all around to see the latest art exhibits and to go to the theater. Busy street markets carried fresh fruits and vegetables and fish—all the food a person would need to feed a family. The city thrived on the very fact that it was a place to gather in public, to meet new and interesting people, and to be a part of the bubbling energy that was Athens. Under the great statesman Pericles (c. 495–429 BCE), Athenian democracy and culture thrived. Its

This illustration shows a reconstruction of the Acropolis, located on a rocky hill in the heart of Athens, Greece. During its golden age, the polis of Athens was a magnet for scholars, craftspeople, and merchants.

centrally located acropolis, atop a walled hill, not only served as a military stronghold but also housed a majestic temple dedicated to Athena, municipal structures, and other religious buildings.

Not surprisingly, Athens, being such an acclaimed cultural center, also managed to attract the brightest intellectuals of the time. The city's force was almost magnetic. Some of the greatest writers, philosophers, and mathematicians in Greece migrated to Athens. They did so for good reason. The atmosphere of a place like Athens could stimulate the mind and move great thinkers to develop new ideas. Intellectuals from all over Greece would gather and talk for hours.

These intellectuals, including philosophers (from the Greek word *philosophos*, for those who "love wisdom"), were guaranteed the right to speak their minds because of the democratic society in which they lived. Greek democracy allowed certain people (not all people), "citizens," liberty in two specific ways. First, they had the political freedom to take part in the democratic process. They could speak at public meetings, vote for new laws or amendments to existing laws, and generally participate in the workings of government. Second, they had the freedom to do what they wished in their private lives. In other words, when among family and friends, or even just acquaintances, they could speak their minds without fear of persecution.

Although this democracy might sound similar to the democracy that people experience today, there were some important differences. One difference was that in Athenian democracy, equality was only guaranteed in politics, not in social or economic life. A poor man who participated in the Athenian democratic process could vote and speak out, but that didn't mean he'd be granted an opportunity to move up in life or to achieve wealth or improved social status. Today, for example, if you're born to a poor family you can probably find opportunities to work your way out of poverty. Chances are you can go to school with the help of grants and loans from the government. Moreover, any career is potentially yours, if you're willing to put in the work to get you there. In ancient Athens, on the other hand, a man on the bottom usually stayed at the bottom.

Another distinction—and by far the most significant distinction—was that not all those who lived in Athens were considered citizens. To have political rights, you had to be a citizen. In early Athens, only adult male residents who weren't slaves were guaranteed citizenship. Women, foreigners, children, and slaves, on the other hand, lacked the political rights of their adult male counterparts.

For those lucky enough to be considered citizens—that is, free men older than the age of eighteen—democracy was an integral part of daily life. Experts today believe there were somewhere around thirty thousand adult males living in Athens during Euclid's time who fell into this category. This number was in a city about the size of Stockton, California, with an overall population of around three hundred thousand.

As it was, Athenian democracy permitted any citizen to speak out at the public assembly. Citizens could also vote at the assemblies, which were typically held several dozen

Pnyx was a hill west of the Acropolis. The Athenian assembly usually met every week here to govern, listen to political leaders speak, and bring matters to a vote for eligible citizens.

times per year on Athens's Pnyx hill. Meetings were held outside in the open air, not far from the Acropolis. Speakers would climb onto a platform called a bema to deliver speeches. These enormous meetings would attract thousands of citizens, many of whom took turns voicing their thoughts about the matters at hand. Everything pertaining to state affairs was discussed, including both domestic and foreign policy initiatives.

After sometimes lengthy discussions and debates, issues were decided by a vote. An individual made his choice known by raising his hand. Hands were counted—or at least estimated—and a final decision was made.

This type of democracy is now known as a direct democracy. Unlike the representative or parliamentary democracies typical of today, the citizens who took part in Athenian democracy directly influenced government. They didn't choose people to represent them at government meetings. They went to those meetings themselves.

ANCIENT GREECE AND SLAVERY

Slaves were common in ancient Greece, so common, in fact, that some historians believe that, in the cities especially, there may have been more slaves than free people.

Slaves came from all walks of life. Some people became slaves as young children, when they were either born into slavery because their parents were slaves or were sold into slavery by their impoverished family. Other children became slaves when they were abandoned as infants by their parents. They would be picked up by a stranger and sold to someone who was wealthy. Once taken in by a rich family, they were destined to a life of servitude.

Other people became slaves when they were captured during war. Ancient Greece was a time of much upheaval, and battles raged for many years. When enemy cities were captured, they were looted by the invading army. Any survivors were forced into a life of slavery.

In a city such as Athens, slaves were everywhere. The wealthiest of families often relied on up to twenty slaves at a time to help them run their households. Other slaves worked as laborers, doing everything from cleaning streets to building and maintaining ships. Anywhere there was work to be done, slaves were there. Almost every job was a slave's job.

This sandstone sculpture represents the Scythian slave who served Apollo and flayed the satyr Marsyas. Greeks believed that slaves were essential for Greece's economy. Slavery was used in architectural projects, agriculture, and domestic work.

Despite the fact that Greek culture was very advanced in some ways, the cruel practice of slavery was widespread. Much of ancient Greece's economy was dependent on the practice of slavery. Although it was not a common practice, slaves could be freed by their owners.

ALEXANDER OF MACEDONIA

The name Alexander the Great has, for more than two thousand years, signified this man's focused quest to conquer and rule the world. While Athens practically overflowed with its new democratic ambitions, the Greek leader Alexander set out to become the greatest conqueror the ancients had ever known.

In Alexander's world, kings ruled over enormous stretches of land. Armies marched hundreds, even thousands, of miles on foot to conquer remote cities and expand their empires. Soldiers could be forced to march for days

This mosaic depicts the Battle of Issus (now in Turkey) in 333 BCE *when Alexander of Macedon* (far left) *defeated King Darius III of Persia (in chariot). The following year, Alexander reached Egypt and was welcomed as pharaoh there.*

over difficult terrain, and many died of exhaustion or malnourishment. It was, however, all for a cause. At that time, it was common for leaders to try to build the largest empire they could.

ALEXANDER AND ALEXANDRIA

After Alexander the Great defeated Egypt, he traveled to an oracle in the Egyptian desert before going to Persia. He imagined a great city that would unite Greece and Egypt. According to Andrew Lawler, in an article in *Smithsonian Magazine* entitled "Raising Alexandria," Alexander selected a location 20 miles (32 kilometers) west of the Nile River. He envisioned 10 miles (16 km) of walls and a network of streets, several nearly 100 feet (30 meters) wide.

Eight years after he established Alexandria, Alexander died in Babylon (present-day Iraq), after succumbing to a fever. Ptolemy I had been given authority over Egypt, and before Alexander's body could be taken back to his homeland of Macedon (Alexander left instructions to be buried at the temple of Zeus Ammon at Siwa Oasis), he brought it to Alexandria where the body was placed in a gold coffin. Ptolemy built a majestic tomb for Alexander, and it was said that people came from near and far to visit it. Years later, according to some scholars, the gold coffin was replaced by one made of alabaster. The Roman emperor Septimius Severus, who ruled from 193 to 211 CE, is thought to have moved Alexander's body to where no one could find it. In 2014, archaeologists discovered a gigantic tomb in northern Greece, in Amphipolis, that dates to the time of Alexander the Great. The site is even larger than the burial site of Philip II, Alexander's father. The remains of five bodies have been found within the boxlike tomb. Some people initially believed that Alexander was buried deep within the tomb; others speculated that the body could be that of a general or a member of his immediate family, perhaps his mother Olympias. Still others doubt any connection to Alexander at all.

Ptolemy fulfilled many of Alexander's dreams for the city of Alexandria and later at the entrance of the harbor began construction of the Pharos, a towering lighthouse of more than 350 feet (110 meters) high, which was regarded as one of the Seven Wonders of the World. Historians believe that the Pharos was completed around 283 BCE.

This ambitious mission was the logic in the ancient kingdom of Macedon, located in approximately the same region as present-day Macedonia, just north of modern Greece. In 359 BCE, Macedon was just one of several kingdoms belonging to ancient Greece, but it was also rapidly becoming the most powerful, and Phillip II was its ruler. But Phillip II's days were numbered, and in 336 BCE he was murdered.

Phillip II had a son, and in ancient Greece, sons of kings succeeded their fathers. Alexander, born in 356 BCE (three years into his father's rule), took the throne at the age of twenty. Alexander picked up right where his father had left off, almost immediately embarking on a campaign to conquer the entire known world. Alexander's forces conquered lands from Egypt in North Africa to parts of present-day India and the Persian Gulf. Thanks to his powerful and relentless army, his holdings grew bigger by the day.

Even the most powerful of rulers eventually dies, and for Alexander, death came early. Medicine at the time was not nearly as effective as it is today, and in 323 BCE, Alexander the Great succumbed to a fever and died. He was just thirty-two.

As Alexander the Great's empire spread across the world, so, too, did all the cultural ideals of Greece. The Classical Age that had once been confined to a relatively small region took hold wherever Alexander, who had been educated in Athens by such great philosophers as Aristotle, and his armies set foot.

Hellenism, as the culture and lifestyle of the time after his death became known, was immensely popular. Greek civilization and everything it represented was growing gradually and steadily. All aspects of progressive Greek life little by little took hold of the world's imagination. People saw promise in Hellenism, perhaps as their ticket to a better future.

THE SUCCESSION OF PTOLEMY

When Alexander died, there was an immediate grab for power. There were many of the former king's *Diadochi*,

This silver tetradrachm coin depicts Alexander wearing an elephant skin headdress. Some believe that the headdress represents Alexander's military conquests in India. The coin was minted in Alexandria during the rule of Ptolemy I Soter, who became king of Egypt after Alexander's death.

or successors. These men included Alexander's top army generals, the men who had led countless soldiers into battle in the name of expanding their leader's empire. Each of the generals believed he deserved to personally rule at least part of the land that was now without a king. Not surprisingly, things quickly became bloody. The struggle for power was ferocious.

One of those to emerge from the carnage was Alexander's topmost general, Ptolemy I (366–282 BCE). Ptolemy I headed for Egypt, and in 304 BCE, he became king of a land whose prize possession was the city of Alexandria, which Alexander the Great had founded in 331 BCE, eight years before his death. (After Ptolemy died, his dynasty ruled in Egypt until 145 BCE).

Alexandria was in an ideal location—it was right on the Mediterranean, nestled between two branches of the beautiful Nile River. The city had yet to be completed, being fairly new, so Ptolemy's first mission was to finish its construction. He did so quickly, employing huge numbers of people to get the work done. When the city was finished, Ptolemy, perhaps in honor of his fallen leader, declared Alexandria Egypt's new capital.

A CENTER OF LEARNING

Ptolemy's vision for the city closely resembled that of Athens, and he set out to make Alexandria one of the world's top educational and scholarly centers. Toward that end, the leader of Egypt built what became known as the Museum or Greek Mouseion ("Seat of Muses").

Unlike the museums of today, which typically offer various themed displays, this gigantic, luxurious complex was designed for teaching and research.

Top students came to the Museum from all over the world. They studied together, went to class together, ate together, and lived together on the Museum's grounds. Surrounded by lavish courts and beautiful gardens, containing libraries stocked with thousands of scrolls of the world's most respected writings, and complete with an adjacent zoo, the Museum quickly became renowned as the primary institution for higher education. Students, many of whom were among the most important intellectuals of the time, not only learned the essential subjects of the day but also taught them. Math, astronomy, science, and medicine were almost everything a man of classical Greece needed to know, and they could all be mastered at the Museum. It was a place for ideas, debate, and progress. It was also the home of a man who many believe was its greatest teacher: Euclid.

CHAPTER TWO

Mathematics in Greece

The word "mathematics" originates from the Greek word meaning "things that have been learned." Mathematics owes much of its progress and development to the intellectuals of ancient Greece's Classical Age. These intellectuals ranged from Thales of Miletus (c. 624–c.547 BCE), who is believed to have invented the subject of geometry (a branch of mathematics that deals with measurements and relationships between points, lines, and shapes) to Pythagoras (c. 570–490 BCE), who more than anyone else managed to make mathematics a subject for the masses. Finally, Euclid took mathematics and geometry to an entirely new level.

But the Greeks did not invent mathematics. That honor goes to the Egyptians. As early as 3000 BCE, the Egyptians had settled into the fertile region of the upper Nile. There, they developed a society in which mathematical calculations

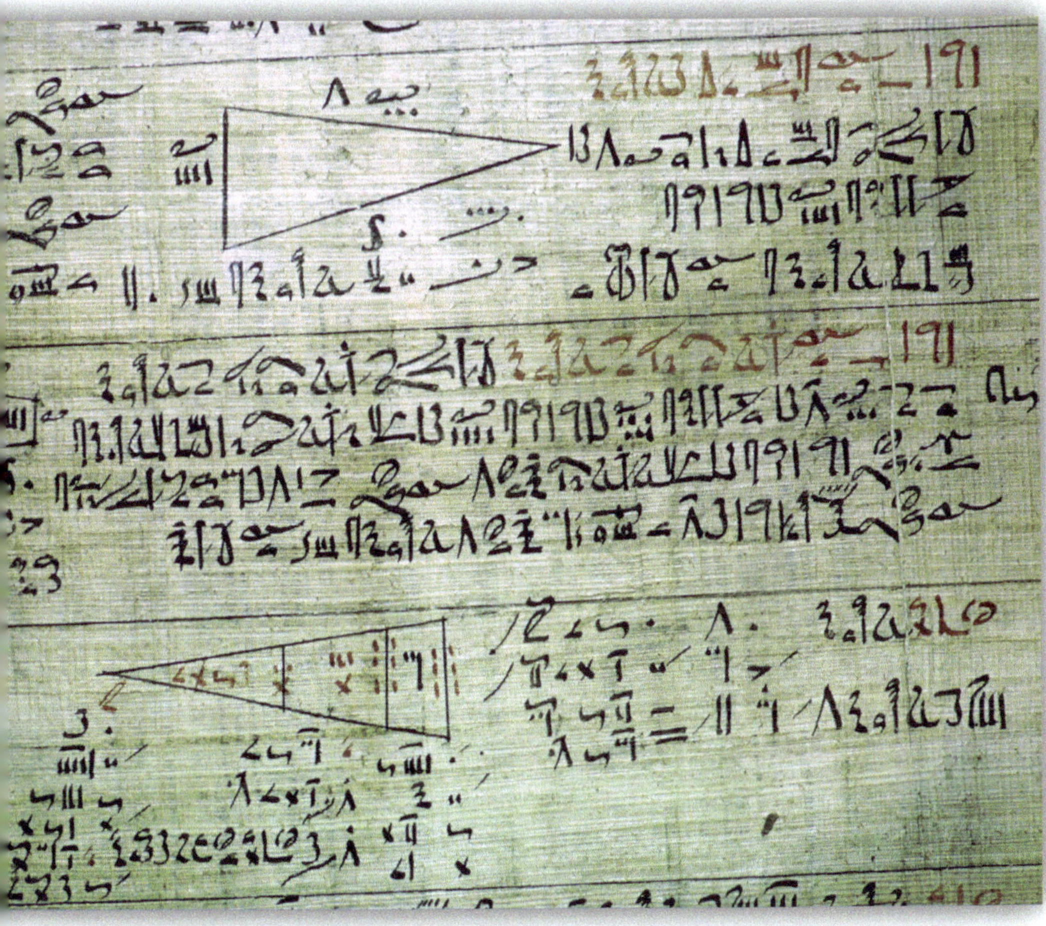

The Rhind mathematical papyrus contains eighty-four problems that involve numerical operations, problem solving, and geometric shapes. It was made in Thebes, Egypt, around 1550 BCE and would have been used by scribes to learn how to solve practical problems.

were necessary for keeping business records, for recording taxes, and for the fair exchange of things such as food, tools, and land. The use of numbers was a logical way to keep track of daily transactions, and before long, addition and subtraction, as well as primitive forms of multiplication and division, were used in everyday life.

Two famous documents, the Rhind and Moscow Papyri, survive from around 1550 BCE and 1850 BCE, respectively, and show evidence of mathematical problems and equations being done. Modern-day historians have learned almost everything they know about Egyptian mathematics from these scrolls.

If the Egyptians invented mathematics, the Greeks revolutionized it. Although ancient Egyptians used numbers in strictly practical ways, seeing them not as symbols but as actual objects, the Greeks used more abstract thinking to develop mathematical ideas. The Greeks moved from performing calculations for specific and practical problems to defining formulas that could be used anywhere. They also invented proofs to verify that their formulas were correct. A proof would begin with a mathematical statement that was known to be true. This statement, using logic and reasoning, would be built upon to eventually ensure that a second statement was also true.

Similarly, the Greeks did not invent geometry. The Egyptians were obviously well acquainted with geometry, otherwise they never would have built pyramids to such complete perfection or understood how land could be measured and divided fairly among various owners. The Babylonians lived in ancient Mesopotamia (a region in southwestern Asia, essentially the same area as modern-day Iraq) in the fertile valley of the lower Euphrates and Tigris Rivers between 1900 and 1600 BCE. Archaeologists have found clay tablets in the region with numbers etched onto them, showing that the Babylonians used math, specifically geometry, to make calculations.

The Greeks did use geometry, however, and they advanced it to a form that is still used today. They used it in everyday life to divide plots of land into rectangles. The price of the plot would depend on its size. They would also use geometry in the construction of homes, courtyards, and public structures to get angles just right or to calculate how tall walls should be. Entire cities were laid out using geometrical principles.

It is believed that many educated Greeks during the Classical Age were adept at using numbers and performing basic calculations, but very few could be considered mathematicians. The true Greek mathematicians were few and far between. It is to those few—the rarest of great thinkers—that modern mathematics truly owes its existence.

THALES OF MILETUS

The history of Greek mathematics and mathematicians begins with Thales of Miletus in Asia Minor (present-day Turkey). Widely considered to be Europe's first philosopher, Thales was also a scientist, an astronomer, and the top geometer of his time. Thales was also regarded as one of the Seven Wise Men of Greece (also called the Seven Sages). The exact date of Thales' birth

Thales was considered by historians to be one of the Seven Wise Men of Greece and the first mathematician to use deductive reasoning in geometry. He is credited with proving five theorems about circles and triangles.

is not known, but he was active in the seventh and sixth centuries BCE.

Although Thales lived in Greece and did well for himself as a businessman and politician in his homeland, he was also restless. He yearned to travel, to learn the ways of the world. With that in mind, he embarked for Egypt.

Thales learned a lot in Egypt, especially from that country's expert builders and surveyors. He saw how the surveyors measured out parcels of land for peasants. The peasants would in turn raise crops on the land and pay taxes to the Egyptian ruler—the pharaoh—as rent. Taxes were levied according to how much land each peasant worked.

Mingling with the Egyptian builders, Thales watched workers using special ropes with knots in them to measure perfect right angles. The knots were spaced at regular intervals along the rope so that the rope could be used as a measuring device. Knowing the relationship between the lengths of the three sides of a right triangle, which includes a right angle (a ninety-degree angle) between two of the sides, men could use the knotted ropes to make buildings with square walls.

Thales also learned how Egyptians used measuring sticks and the shadows those sticks cast in the sunlight to determine the height of large buildings or monuments. These calculations, too, required an understanding of triangles and the relationships between a triangle's three sides.

Thales was amazed by what he learned in Egypt. He was eager to bring his discoveries back with him to Greece and to teach what he had learned to others. Upon his return, Thales opened a school. Students flocked to him from across the Mediterranean region to learn a new subject: geometry.

The word "geometry" is from the Greek words meaning "land measurement." Thales also invented a unique way of teaching this subject. He used logic and reason, in a systematic, step-by-step fashion, to prove the mathematical principles he used. Greek geometry, founded on the work of the builders of ancient Egypt and adapted slightly for new uses, was born.

PYTHAGORAS OF SAMOS

One of Thales' top students was a man named Pythagoras from the Greek island of Samos. Born around 570 BCE, Pythagoras learned everything he could from Thales before deciding to move on. He traveled to Egypt, where he studied geometry and astronomy. He then continued on to Babylon and many other parts of the world before returning to the Greek colony of Croton to found a new school.

The primary subject Pythagoras taught at his school was geometry. Like Thales, Pythagoras used logic to build on what he already knew was true. In this way, he could derive new theorems from ones that were already proven. He used diagrams etched into the dirt or constructed with pebbles to help him visualize his work. Only rarely did he use papyrus sheets for writing, as the material was very expensive and hard to come by.

II

primi:quadratis duaꝝ linearum.c.b.z.b.a.ergo dempto ab vtrisq3 quadrato li/nee.c.b.erit qd̄ fit ex.d.f.in.b.f.z ipsū est superficies.d.g.equale quadrato linee a.b.ergo dempto ab vtrisq3 paralelogramo.b.d.erit quadratū.b.f.equale palello gramo.b.c.z quia quadratum.b.f.est quadratum linee.b.b.z palellogramū.b.c. producitur ex.c.a.que est equalis.a.b.in.a.b.patet factum esse propositū. ¶Ad hoc autē faciendum in numeris non labores:quia impossibile est numerum sic di/uidi:vt hic vndecima proponit sicut scies sexti.29.te docente.

Propositio .12.

In his triangulis qui obtusum habent angulum: tanto ea que obtusum subtendit angulum:ambobus reliquis lateribus que obtusum continent angulum amplius potest.quā tū est qd̄ cōtinet bis sub vno eoꝝ:atq3 ea que sibi directe iūcta ad obtusum angulū a ppēdiculari extra dephendit.

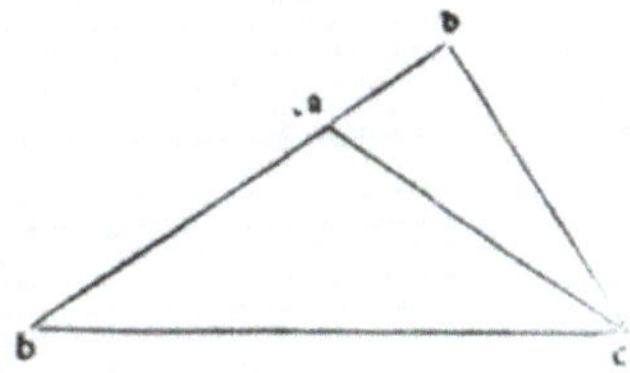

¶Sit triangulus.a.b.c.habens angulum.a.obtusum.a puncto.c.ducat linea p/pendicularis ad lineā.b.a.que necessario cadet extra triangulū.a.b.c. alioqn an/gulus obtusus esset rectus aut minor recto p.16.primi:sit ergo.c.d. perpendicula ris super lineam.a.b. productam vsq3 ad.d. Dico ꝙ quadratum lateris.b.c.qd̄ subtenditur angulo obtuso tanto maius est duabus quadratis duarum linearum a.b.z.a.c.ambientibus ipsum angulum obtusum.quantum est illud qd̄ fit ex.b.a.in.a.d.bis: potentia enī linee respectu q̄drati sui est.vnde tm̄ dicit posse linea quelibet quantū in se ducta produci.Erit enī p.4.hui⁹ q̄dratū.b.d.equale duo/bus quadratis duarum linearum.b.a.z.a.d.z duplo eius qd̄ fit ex.b.a.in.a.d.et quia quadratum.b.c.per penultimam primi est equale quadrato.b.d.z quadrato d.c.ipsum erit equale quadratis trium linearum.b.a.a.d.z.d.c. z duplo eius qd̄ fit ex.b.a.i.a.d.sed p candē quadratū.a.c.ē equale quadratis.a.d.z.d.c.ergo q̄/dratum.b.c.est equale quadratis duarum linearum.b.a.z.c.a.z duplo eius qd̄ fit ex.b.a.in.a.d.quare.b.c.tanto amplius potest duabus lineis.b.a.a.c. quantum est duplū eius.qd̄ fit ex.b.a.in.a.d. Jam enim diximus ꝙ tantū dicitur posse li/nea quelibet quantum in se ducta producit quod est propositum.

Propositio .13.

Omnis oxigonij tanto ea que acutum respicit angulū ambobus lateribus angulum acutum continentibus minus potest:quātum est qd̄ bis continetur sub vno eorum cui ppendicularis intra superstat:eaq3 sui parte:que perpendiculari anguloq3 acuto interiacet.

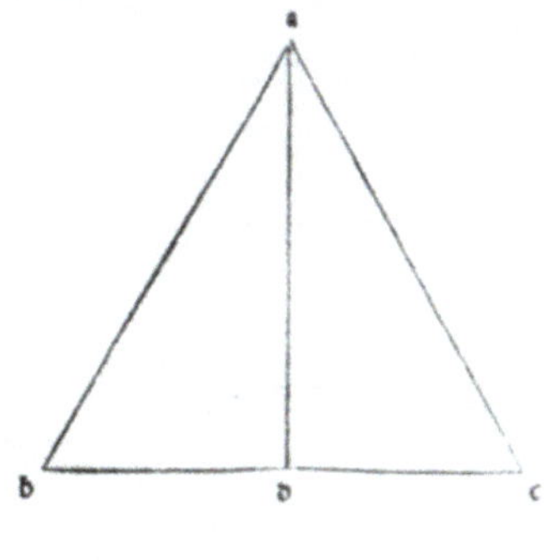

¶Quod hic proponitur de latere subteuso alicui angulo acuto in triangulo oxi/gonio veritatem habet de latere subtenso cuilibet angulo acuto in omni triangu/lo siue fiat orthogonius siue ambligoni⁹ siue oxigonius. ¶Sit ergo in triangulo a.b.c.quicūq3 triangulus fuerit.angulus.c.acutus qui si fuerit oxigonius ducatur ppendicularis ab vtroq3 anguloꝝ.a.vel.b.ad vtrāq3 basim.b.c.vel.a.c.quia cum sic fuerit semper cadet perpendicularis intra triangulum.Si autem sit ambligo/nius aut orthogonius ab angulo obtuso vel recto ducatur perpendicularis ad latus oppositū quā manifestū est cadere intra triangulū:z ut simpliciter dicam cum in omni triangulo sunt duo acuti anguli necessario erit alter reliquoꝝ angulorū. qui sunt.a.z.b.acutus.Ducam igitur perpendicularē ad lineam illam que duobus

b 4

This page, which is written in Latin, from a 1482 Venetian edition of Euclid's Elements, *Book II, Propositions (or "postulates") 12 and 13, includes a geometric diagram about an obtuse angle and one of an acute angle. These postulates supplement the Pythagorean theorem for right triangles that Euclid discussed in Book I, postulate 47.*

Pythagoras's most famous contribution to geometry was the so-called Pythagorean theorem, about which Euclid later wrote. The theorem explains the relationships between the three sides of a right triangle. Interestingly, the Pythagorean theorem was not new. The Babylonians had used this very theorem nearly two thousand years earlier. Even the Egyptians whom Thales visited had unknowingly used the theorem when they used knotted ropes to measure right angles. Pythagoras merely devised a way to prove that the relationships between a triangle's sides are always the same. His formula was $a_2 + b_2 = c_2$. The letters *a*, *b*, and *c* refer to the length of each of the triangle's three sides. Side *a* multiplied by itself plus side *b* multiplied by itself equals side *c* multiplied by itself. This formula is incredibly useful in figuring out certain lengths.

Pythagoras's students were so intrigued by the man and his mathematical abilities that they formed the Pythagorean Order, an exclusive and secret group that followed him and his teachings almost religiously. This group of people, which included members from around the known world, were said to pursue mathematical knowledge for knowledge's sake alone. They believed it was their duty to teach the things they learned.

PLATO AND HIS ACADEMY

Sometime after Pythagoras, around 428 BCE, Plato was born. Unlike Pythagoras, Plato, who lived in Athens, was primarily a philosopher, not a mathematician. He spent his days thinking about life, what it meant to exist, the differences between reality and imagination, and the differences between right and wrong. Still, he knew enough about mathematics to realize that it was an important part of any education.

Like the greats who came before him, Plato, who was initially tutored by Socrates—a great philosopher known for his rational thinking and emphasis on logic—gained much of his education while traveling around the Mediterranean region. He learned everything he could about the subjects of the day. When he finally made his way back home to Athens around 387 BCE, he was determined to open his own school.

Plato's school became known as the Academy, and it earned a reputation as a renowned institution for the study of philosophy, law, science, astronomy, music, and mathematics. For all practical purposes, Plato's contribution to mathematics ended here. The reason for this was that math was considered important at his school, but it was just one of several subjects he expected his students to master. Today, Plato's take on geometry continues to exemplify his complicated thoughts about existence and reality. Plato saw geometrical figures as ideal forms for their precision. To him, such geometrical shapes were absolutely perfect and unchanging. When such figures were found in everyday life—such as circular objects in nature, for example—he recognized that these representations of the perfect geometrical shapes were fleeting. They didn't last forever and were far from perfect in form. Plato's Academy and its influence lasted until about 529

CE, when the Byzantine emperor Justinian closed it along with other non-Christian institutions.

In this nineteenth-century watercolor, Plato teaches some of his students in the olive grove of the Academy. Plato expected his students to master mathematics along with natural science and dialectics (a type of reasoning), among other subjects.

EUDOXUS OF CNIDUS

One of Plato's students at the Academy was a man by the name of Eudoxus, who was born around 395 BCE in Cnidus, Asia Minor (which is in present-day Turkey), and died around 342 BCE. Eudoxus, like those before him, traveled extensively as a young man, hoping to learn from people he met in distant parts of the world. He took a particular liking to astronomy and invented mathematical formulas to explain the movements of the planets and stars.

Eudoxus eventually became well known, both as a mathematics teacher and for his theory of proportions. Euclid discussed this theory some time later in *Elements*, a geometry textbook that for more than two thousand years served as the definitive reference for students new to the

Aristotle studied with Plato for nearly twenty years before opening his own school, called the Lyceum, in Athens. A philosopher and scientist, Aristotle employed mathematical methods in his logic and philosophical works.

subject. Eudoxus also developed a theory involving concentric spheres. This theory held that Earth was rooted in the center of the universe and that everything else in space, no matter how far away from Earth, revolved around it in concentric orbits. Of course, since Euclid's time, his theory of concentric spheres has been proven incorrect. Today's astronomers know that Earth is just one of many planets and other bodies in the universe that orbit the sun.

ARISTOTLE

Another of Plato's students, and easily his most famous, was Aristotle, who lived from 384 to 322 BCE. Although Aristotle was among the youngest of the students at the Academy, he was also one of the most promising. Known as a great philosopher, Aristotle spent much of his life in deep thought, asking questions about life and existence, and proposing answers based on experience and reason.

After leaving the Academy, Aristotle taught in Asia Minor and studied marine biology on the island of Lesbos. Philip II of Macedonia asked Aristotle to teach his son, Alexander, at the Macedonian court. Later, when he because king of Macedonia, Alexander supported Aristotle financially in setting up a school, called the Lyceum, in Athens. Aristotle went on to write and philosophize from the Lyceum. He also taught various subjects at the school, including astronomy, physics, logic, and math. Although he was not a mathematician in the strict sense of the word, he was, like many intellectuals in the Classical Age of Greece, interested in mathematics and how numbers helped explain the workings of the world. He saw beauty in math and knew that it was an essential component of any classical education. More important, Aristotle was a key figure in the culture of philosophical investigation into which Euclid was born. The work of Aristotle, Plato, and other great Greek thinkers helped pave the way for Euclid's great contributions to mathematics.

CHAPTER THREE

The Life of Euclid

Scholars know very little about the personal life of Euclid. Because of a scarcity of paper and a culture in which teaching and learning most often occurred through oral communication, relatively few historical documents exist from the days of ancient Greece. Without such documents, much of what historians can conclude about Euclid amounts to little more than an educated guess.

To make matters even more difficult for historians, the name "Euclid" was very common in ancient Greece. Therefore the texts that have been recovered must be read carefully. When the name "Euclid" is mentioned in writing, it's often in reference to other Euclids from the same time period. In fact, some scholars have mistakenly drawn false conclusions about the most famous Euclid. They thought they were

Historians do not know much about the personal life of Euclid. No known depictions of his true physical appearance have survived.

reading about the mathematician when, in fact, they were reading about someone else. Perhaps the best known—other than the author of *Elements*—was Euclid of Megara. A philosopher from the days of Plato, Euclid of Megara's legacy became forever entwined with that of the author Euclid hundreds of years after both of them were dead. It seems that translators attempting to decipher the ancient text of *Elements* and the commentaries written about it mistook a reference to Euclid of Alexandria for a reference to Euclid of Megara. As a result, Euclid of Megara was temporarily given credit for *Elements*, the greatest geometry book ever written.

Although the name "Euclid" was very popular during the geometer's time, that hasn't prevented some historians from speculating on its origins or from making wild assumptions. Some authors, for instance, claim it was derived from the Arabic words *ucli* and *dis*, which mean "key" and "measurement," respectively. Did the name "Euclid" really mean "the key to measurement"? Or even better, "the key to geometry"? Considering that Euclid was Greek, and not Arab, it's highly unlikely. If it did mean that, however, one could definitely say Euclid lived up to his name.

There was another problem. When Euclid did write, he never wrote about himself. Often authors will include at least a preface, or short introductory section, that provides a background for their work and offers information about their lives. This was not so with Euclid. Euclid's surviving books contain no hints about his personal life. In addition, the great philosophers and teachers of the time, including

THE PHILOSOPHER PROCLUS

Much of the personal information historians know about Euclid comes directly from the work of the philosopher Proclus. Proclus, who was also a mathematician, was born around 410 CE in Constantinople and died in Athens in 485, almost 800 years after Euclid. Proclus wrote a commentary on Euclid's most famous book, *Elements*. Here's what he wrote, as quoted in *A History of Greek Mathematics*, translated from the Greek:

> Euclid . . . put together the *Elements*, collecting many of Eudoxus's theorems, perfecting many of Theaetetus's, and also bringing to irrefragable demonstration the things which were only somewhat loosely proved by his predecessors. This man lived in the time of the first Ptolemy. For Archimedes, who came immediately after the first (Ptolemy), makes mention of Euclid . . . He is then younger than the pupils of Plato, but older than Eratosthenes and Archimedes, the latter having been contemporaries, as Eratosthenes somewhere says.

Sound complicated? It is. Proclus mentions a lot of names in that passage. What he's doing, though, is using a bit of logic to determine when Euclid lived. Proclus notes that Euclid was younger than Plato's students, so he must have lived sometime after Plato. He says Euclid is older than Archimedes, so he must have lived before that famous mathematician. Finally, Proclus writes that Euclid lived in the "time of the first Ptolemy." Because historians know that Ptolemy I took over Egypt after Alexander the Great's death in 323 BCE, Euclid had to have been alive at that time, somewhere around 300 BCE.

It's difficult to say just how accurate Proclus was in his estimations of Euclid's lifespan. Like modern-day historians, Proclus was using very old documents and artifacts to discover clues about his subject. In this case, he had read the works of both Plato and Archimedes, as well as Euclid's *Elements*, and used all those documents to make an educated guess about Euclid's life. Just imagine doing the same now for someone who lived nearly eight hundred years ago, around 1215 CE. It wouldn't be an easy task, and it would certainly involve a lot of guesswork.

Still, Proclus's writings are all historians really have to guide them through Euclid's life. Beyond that, much of what they have is even less of a sure thing and therefore must be viewed with some skepticism.

Euclid, used papyrus for their writings. Thanks to Alexander the Great's conquest of Egypt in the fourth century BCE, much of the papyrus writing that survives today is in Greek. Because papyrus scrolls can easily be destroyed, however, many works from ancient times that might have shed light on Euclid's life have been lost.

For these reasons, Euclid remains somewhat of an enigma. He was a Greek mathematician who flourished in Alexandria, Egypt, around 300 BCE. His specialty was geometry, and he was known as a great teacher, perhaps the greatest of his time. He wrote *Elements* (in Greek, *Stoicheia*) along with a half dozen other book and may or may not have written several more. And then, on a date that can only be guessed, and for a reason that no one will probably ever know, he died.

EUCLID, THE STUDENT

Most of the great philosophers and mathematicians of ancient Greece started out as students. They studied under the respected teachers of their time and then left for a while to travel and learn from other great teachers around the world. Euclid is thought to have taken the same course. Experts today believe that anyone who wished to study mathematics in 300 BCE would have to have done so in Athens, as that was the only place to find textbooks on the subject. Furthermore, in

In this detail from Raphael's fresco entitled The School of Athens *(1509), which is located in the Stanza della Segnatura at the Vatican in Rome, Italy, Euclid, as a teacher, is shown bending over a tablet and using a compass (a tool used in drawing circles).*

Athens there were only two schools where a mathematician of Euclid's caliber could have learned everything he did: Plato's Academy and Aristotle's Lyceum.

The Academy, remember, was the school that Plato founded around 387 BCE. As the philosopher Proclus concluded in his commentary on Euclid's *Elements*, Euclid was younger than the students of Plato. So one can only assume that Euclid did not have Plato himself as his teacher but instead was educated by Plato's followers.

The Academy was a vast complex just outside of Athens. It was named in honor of the ancient Greek war hero Academos, who is said to have owned the land on which the Academy was built. Surrounded by thick stone walls, the Academy served as a public garden and was frequented by people interested in its many statues and temples to the Greek gods or by the peace and tranquility provided by the olive trees that grew within it.

Plato's school was merely one part of the larger Academy. Based in a garden area within the Academy walls, the school became the area's top institution for the study of science and philosophy. Students who studied there had access to the Academy's athletic fields, library, a dining room where they shared meals, and the many gardens that could be found on the grounds.

Euclid would have studied all the subjects taught at the Academy, not just mathematics and geometry. Astronomy, which focused on the planets and planetary movement, as well as the paths of all the stars that could be seen from the school's observatory, was one popular subject. Others included music, science, and debate.

Mathematics was Euclid's favorite subject, and he soon found himself fascinated by geometry. As Proclus said, Euclid studied the geometry of Eudoxus and Theaetetus (c. 417–369 BCE; another philosopher and geometer), both of whom had attended the Academy before him. Euclid later included references to their work in his *Elements*. The fact that the geometry of Eudoxus and Theaetetus was included in *Elements* is one of the reasons historians believe Euclid studied at the Academy.

Euclid is believed to have completely submerged himself in geometry at the Academy, proving himself a devoted and tireless student. Eventually, however, he found he had learned all that he could. One day, while still a young man, he packed up and moved on.

EUCLID, THE TEACHER

Finished with his studies at the Academy, Euclid left Athens and moved to Alexandria, Egypt. Historians are uncertain why Euclid moved to Alexandria. However, the city was a magnet for intellectuals at the time, and it only made sense for people like Euclid, who wished to learn from and converse with other great minds, to call it home.

Soon after Euclid settled into Alexandria he started his own school. Not much is known about Euclid's school, not even its name. What is known is that Euclid wrote *Elements* shortly after he opened the school, and the primary subject taught at the school was mathematics.

Elements soon gained a reputation as the best geometry textbook available. Anyone who hoped to master the

THEAETETUS

The Athenian mathematician Theaetetus was born around 417 BCE and died around 369 BCE.

Most scholars agree that Theaetetus had a major impact on the development of Greek geometry and that Plato admired him immensely. In fact, most of what is known today about Theaetetus comes from two of Plato's dialogues (*Theaetetus* and *Sophist*), in which he was the major subject. Theaetetus was a student of mathematician Theodorus of Cyrene, who, it is said, encouraged him to work on incommensurables. According to *The Britannica Guide to Geometry*, Euclid compiled Theaetetus's contributions in *Elements*, a principal area of which was

> on incommensurables (which correspond to irrational numbers in modern mathematics), in which he extended the work of Theodorus by devising the basic classification of incommensurable magnitudes into different types that is found in Book X of the *Elements*. He also discovered methods of inscribing in a sphere the five Platonic solids (tetrahedron, cube, octahedron, dodecahedron, and icosahedron), the subject of Book XII of the *Elements*.

> Through his systemization of his predecessors' knowledge about geometry in *Elements*, including that of Theaetetus, Euclid enabled generations of math students to learn about the ancients' achievements and therefore build on them.

subject had to have a copy. To get one, however, he had to transcribe the entire text by hand, line by line.

Not long after Euclid founded his school in Alexandria, Ptolemy I built the Museum, the first national university of Egypt. Ptolemy knew that for the Museum to have any credibility as a great institution for learning, he had to have the best teachers. Consequently, familiar with *Elements* and captivated by how clearly it demonstrated the latest developments in geometry, he decided to hire Euclid. Euclid became the Museum's very first professor of mathematics.

Likely the recipient of a respectable salary for his time, Euclid moved to the Museum and settled in with the other great teachers of the day. Along with their students, they lived, ate, did research, and shared ideas with one another. They spent long periods of time in deep thought, perhaps debating each other's theories and ideas. They spent hours in the Museum's great library, deeply absorbed in the vast collection of ancient texts stored on its shelves. The library is believed to have held more than six hundred thousand papyrus rolls. Scholars came to the Museum from all over the world to reference these scrolls and to use them in their studies.

These parchment pages are from a ninth-century Greek translation of Euclid's The Elements, *Book I, postulate 47. The Pythagorean theorem is put forward here: In a right-angled triangle the square on the hypotenuse is equal to the sum of the squares on the other two sides.*

Euclid quickly gained a reputation among his students and colleagues as an exceptional geometry teacher. His lectures grew increasingly popular as word spread of their quality. One day, as recounted in the writings of Proclus, Ptolemy himself sat in on one of Euclid's classes. He listened to what Euclid had to say. Then, according to *A History of Greek Mathematics*, wondering if perhaps there was an easier way to learn geometry, Ptolemy asked Euclid "if there was in geometry any shorter way than that of the *Elements*." Euclid replied that there was "no royal road to geometry."

Another legend, recounted by Stobaeus, a Greek philosopher writing sometime around 500 CE, tells of one of Euclid's students asking his teacher a tough question. As retold in David Berlinski's *The King of Infinite Space: Euclid and His Elements* (2013), the student "asked innocently enough what profit he might gain from studying geometry. Euclid demanded that a slave give the student a few coins, 'since he must make gain out of what he learns.'"

As these two stories show, Euclid must have been a good teacher, and he also must have had a good sense of humor. He challenged his students to work hard, to take the long road and not look for shortcuts. He evidently believed that anyone who hoped to master geometry had to be willing to put in the time, to devote himself to the task. If you needed money as motivation to learn, perhaps you were in the wrong field. Geometers were not wealthy.

Historians have also concluded that Euclid was probably a fair and honest man. These traits are shown in his *Elements*, where he gives credit to both Eudoxus and Theaetetus for their indirect contributions to the book. Much of the information Euclid includes in *Elements*, in fact, is derived from the work of those who came before him. He acknowledges this, demonstrating a respect for others and a willingness to share the intellectual spotlight. Euclid apparently knew that he would never have achieved what he did without the help and contributions of those who came before him. According to Berlinski in *The King of Infinite Space*, "As a mathematician, Euclid took from his predecessors, men such as Eudoxus and Theaetetus, and gave to his successors, Apollonius and Archimedes."

ARCHIMEDES: EUCLID'S MOST ACCLAIMED STUDENT

It's often said that a teacher's skill can be measured by the success of his or her students. If this is so, then Euclid may have been one of the best teachers ever.

Euclid, while working at the school he founded in Alexandria, is believed to have taught Archimedes, who later became known as one of the greatest Greek mathematicians. Archimedes was born around 287 BCE in the Greek colony of Syracuse. He then moved to Alexandria as a young man to attend school. Not much is known about Archimedes' school days, but many historians assume that he became fluent in the fundamentals of mathematics under the tutelage of Euclid. Euclid likely taught Archimedes everything he knew about geometry and perhaps even encouraged him to read his books on that and other subjects.

After Archimedes finished his academic career in Alexandria, he moved back to Syracuse. There he quickly gained a reputation as the "great geometer" and one of the most skillful mathematicians of his time. He was known for his inventions, including levers and pulleys that relied on the laws of physics to allow a single person to move exceedingly heavy objects. He allegedly devised a machine for raising water, which is now known as Archimedes screw. Modern screw pumps are said to be derived from this early device. He made great discoveries in geometry, finding, for example, ways to derive the areas of a variety of geometric shapes.

One story recalls how Archimedes came upon what today is called Archimedes' principle. Archimedes' principle states that a body immersed wholly or partially in a fluid is buoyed up by a force equal in magnitude to the weight of the volume of fluid it displaces. Archimedes had been asked by the king, King Hieron II of Syracuse,

Archimedes was believed to have been one of Euclid's students in Alexandria. He became a distinguished mathematician, inventor, scientist, astronomer, and writer of mathematical treatises.

whether his crown had been made of pure gold, as he was told, or a mixture of gold and some other, cheaper metal, as he suspected he was being cheated.

Archimedes spent many hours searching for a way to figure out the answer to the king's question, but to no avail. Then one day, the solution came to him as he lowered himself into his bathtub. As his body entered the tub, he noticed how the water level around him rose. His body was displacing water in proportion to his body's size. He had discovered the relationship between density and volume, a relationship that would let him determine whether the crown was pure gold. If he knew how much an object weighed, and also knew its volume, he could calculate density (density equals mass divided by volume). By comparing the density of something known to be pure gold with the calculated density of the crown, he could instantly tell if the crown was pure gold, as all pure gold must have the same density. As a result, he proved that the crown was, in fact, not pure gold and that the king was being cheated.

Archimedes died in 212 BCE, during a Roman invasion of his hometown. His legend, however, lives on.

EUCLID'S LEGACY

In *Elements*, one does not find clues about Euclid's life, but one does find evidence of his genius. By looking at some of Euclid's other, lesser-known works, including *Data, Division of Figures, Phaenomena*, and *Optics*, hopefully, one can gain some idea of what each of these texts did to advance science and mathematics. Something can also be learned about Euclid's mind. Euclid was an explorer, a man unafraid to step into the unknown. He took his subject, which he had mastered, to new heights. He did more for geometry and the understanding of geometry than anyone before him or, some say, anyone who followed. By writing *The Elements*, the definitive work on geometry, he explained the subject for all who cared to become proficient in it.

CHAPTER FOUR

EUCLID'S *ELEMENTS* AND OTHER WORKS

Euclid would probably not be known were it not for his greatest and most famous work, *Elements*. As stated in *The King of Infinite Space*, "The Euclid of the *Elements* is stern, logical, unrelenting, a man able to concentrate the powers of his mind on what is abstract and remote." It is unclear when, exactly, Euclid wrote *Elements*. In fact, the original copy of the book is lost.

What is clear, though, is that the book, written on nothing more than a papyrus scroll, changed the subject of geometry forever. *Elements*, widely considered a work of genius unlike any mathematical text that came before it, took a vast and disorganized array of geometric progress accumulated over hundreds of years and brought it all together into one clear and concise work. It made geometry much easier to understand. But

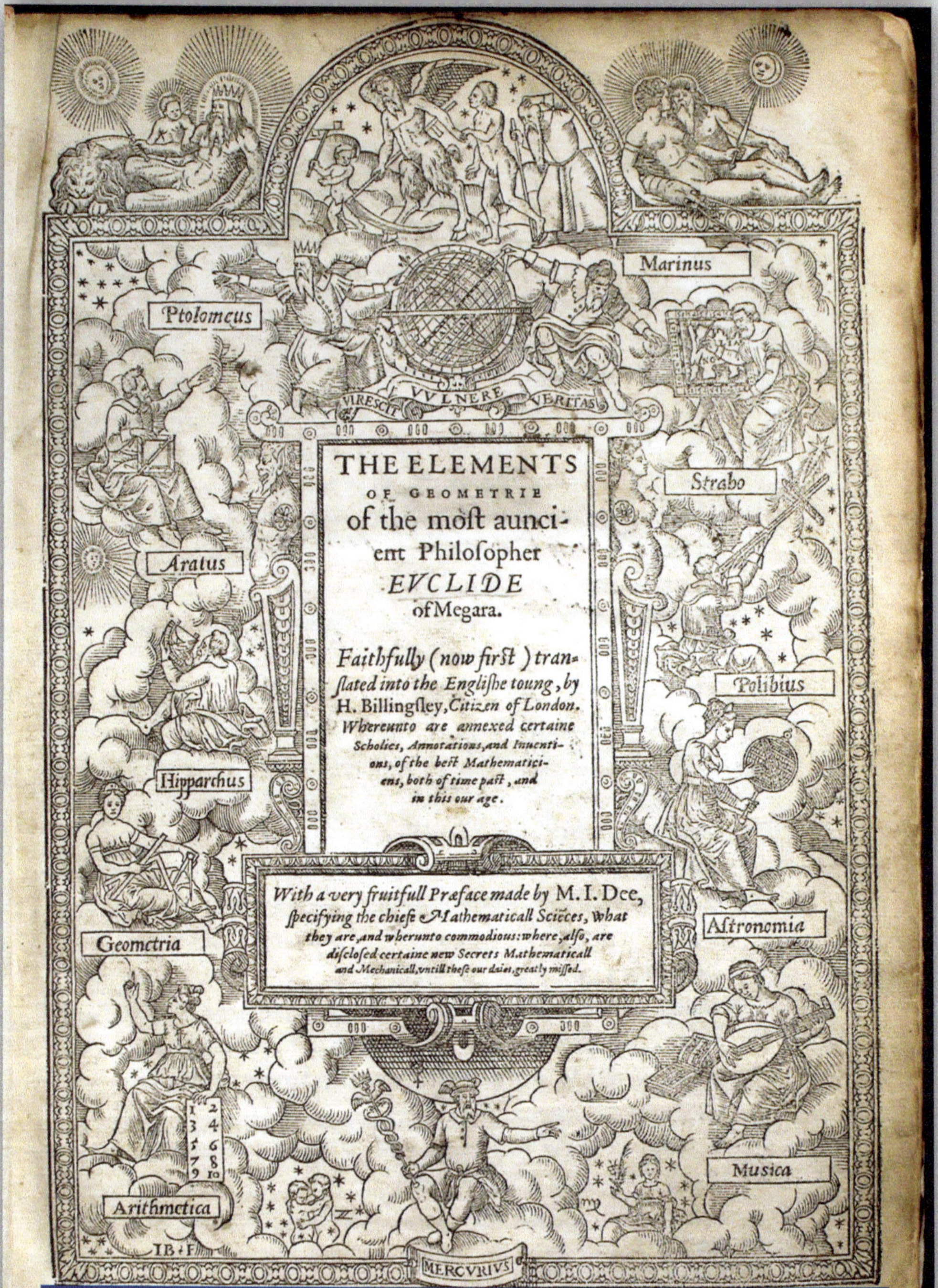

The first English translation of Euclid's Elements *was published in 1570. Sir Henry Billingsley, the Lord Mayor of London, translated it from the Greek, and John Dee, an acclaimed mathematician of the time, wrote the volume's preface about the importance of mathematical studies during the Renaissance.*

even more important, it introduced an entirely new way of presenting complicated information through its unique structure.

Because the original copy of *Elements* is missing, it's impossible to know for sure what was in the original text.

The copies that exist today are translated versions of other copies made hundreds of years ago. They include translations from Greek to Latin, then to Arabic, back to Greek, and then to the Latin of the Middle Ages. (According to many scholars, the earliest manuscript in existence that comes closest to Euclid's original text is the so-called Vatican Euclid, which is a version of a Greek text that dates from the tenth century CE. It was discovered in the Vatican library in 1809 when Napoleon Bonaparte's troops were invading Rome.) Euclid's students couldn't run out to the bookstore and purchase an official copy of *Elements* for class. If they wanted the book, they probably had to sit down and copy the original by hand. This undertaking would have been very tedious work. Some students may have cut corners, perhaps just taking down the information they thought they needed. It's no surprise, then, that most experts believe the compilation *Elements* of today is likely very different from the one Euclid wrote more than two thousand years ago.

BUILDING ON A FIRM FOUNDATION

Euclid's idea to take everything that was known about geometry and organize it to make it clear and easy to follow was

Preclarissimus liber elementorum Euclidis perspi/cacissimi: in artem Geometrie incipit quã foelicissime:

Punctus est cuius ps nõ est. ¶ Linea est lõgitudo sine latitudine cuiꝰ quidẽ ex/tremitates sũt duo pũcta. ¶ Linea recta ẽ ab vno pũcto ad aliũ breuissima extẽ/sio i extremitates suas vtrũq3 eoꝝ reci piens. ¶ Superficies ẽ q̃ lõgitudinẽ ⁊ lati tudinẽ tñ hꝫ: cuiꝰ termi quidẽ sũt linee. ¶ Superficies plana ẽ ab vna linea ad a/liã extẽsio i extremitates suas recipiẽs ¶ Angulus planus ẽ duarũ linearũ al/ternus ꝯtactus: quaꝝ expãsio ẽ sup sup/ficiẽ applicatioq3 nõ directa. ¶ Quãdo aut angulum ꝯtinẽt due linee recte rectilineꝰ angulus noiat. ¶ Qñ recta linea sup rectã steterit duoq3 anguli vtrobiq3 fuerit eq̃les: eoꝝ vterq3 rectꝰ erit ¶ Lineaq3 linee supstãs ei cui supstat ppendicularis vocat. ¶ Angulus vo qui recto maior ẽ obtusus dicit. ¶ Angulꝰ vo minor recto acutꝰ appellat. ¶ Terminꝰ ẽ qd vniuscuiusq3 finis ẽ. ¶ Figura ẽ q̃ tmino vl termis ꝯtinet. ¶ Circulꝰ ẽ figura plana vna q̃dem li/nea ꝯtẽta: q̃ circũferentia noiat: in cuiꝰ medio pũctꝰ ẽ: a quo oẽs linee recte ad circũferẽtiã exeũtes sibiinuicẽ sut equales. Et hic quidẽ pũctꝰ cẽtrũ circuli dr. ¶ Diameter circuli ẽ linea recta que sup eiꝰ centꝝ trãsiens extremitatesq3 suas circũferẽtie applicans circulũ i duo media diuidit. ¶ Semicirculus ẽ figura plana dia/metro circuli ⁊ medietate circũferentie ꝯtenta. ¶ Portio circu/li ẽ figura plana recta linea ⁊ parte circũferẽtie ꝯtẽta: semicircu/lo quidẽ aut maior aut minor. ¶ Rectilinee figure sũt q̃ rectis li/neis cõtinent quarũ quedã trilatere q̃ tribꝰ rectis lineis: quedã quadrilatere q̃ qtuor rectis lineis. q̃dã mltilatere que pluribus q3 quatuor rectis lineis continent. ¶ Figurarũ trilaterarũ: alia est triangulus hñs tria latera equalia. Alia triangulus duo hñs eq̃lia latera. Alia triangulus triũ inequalium laterũ. Haꝝ iterũ alia est orthogoniũ: vnũ. s. rectum angulum habens. Alia ẽ am/bligonium aliquem obtusum angulum habens. Alia est oxigoni um: in qua tres anguli sunt acuti. ¶ Figurarũ autẽ quadrilateraꝝ Alia est q̃dratum quod est equilaterũ atq3 rectangulũ. Alia est tetragonꝰ longꝰ: q̃ est figura rectangula: sed equilatera non est. Alia est helmuaym: que est equilatera: sed rectangula non est.

De principijs p se notis: ⁊ pmo de diffini tionibus earundem.

This page is from the first edition of Elements, *printed in Latin in 1482. It was supposedly based on a translation from the Arabic made by Abelard of Bath in the twelfth century. Erhard Ratdolt, a German printer, worked in Venice, Italy, when he published this edition. He was able to work out how to print geometric diagrams.*

not new. In fact, other geometers had already tried it. But the task was huge, and Euclid succeeded where the others failed.

What did Euclid do differently from those who came before him? He started from scratch. He took the most basic ideas—the same ideas others had often ignored—and then built upon them. He approached geometry like a carpenter might approach a house. He began with the foundation, made sure it was solid, then built in stages from there. When he was through, his "house," his *Elements*, stood strong.

THE THIRTEEN BOOKS OF *THE ELEMENTS*

Euclid wrote *Elements* in thirteen separate books, each of which tackled a different aspect of geometry. Each book was laid out in similar fashion. To understand how *Elements* was organized, you can look at Book I, which is about plane geometry. Plane geometry deals with plane figures, that is, objects with flat surfaces.

Book I begins with a series of simple definitions. Some of these definitions (as they appear in *The Thirteen Books of Euclid's Elements*, by Euclid,) you may already have heard of, especially if you've had any exposure to geometry:

1. A point is that which has no part.
2. A line is breadthless length.
3. The extremities of a line are points.
4. A straight line is a line which lies evenly with points on itself.

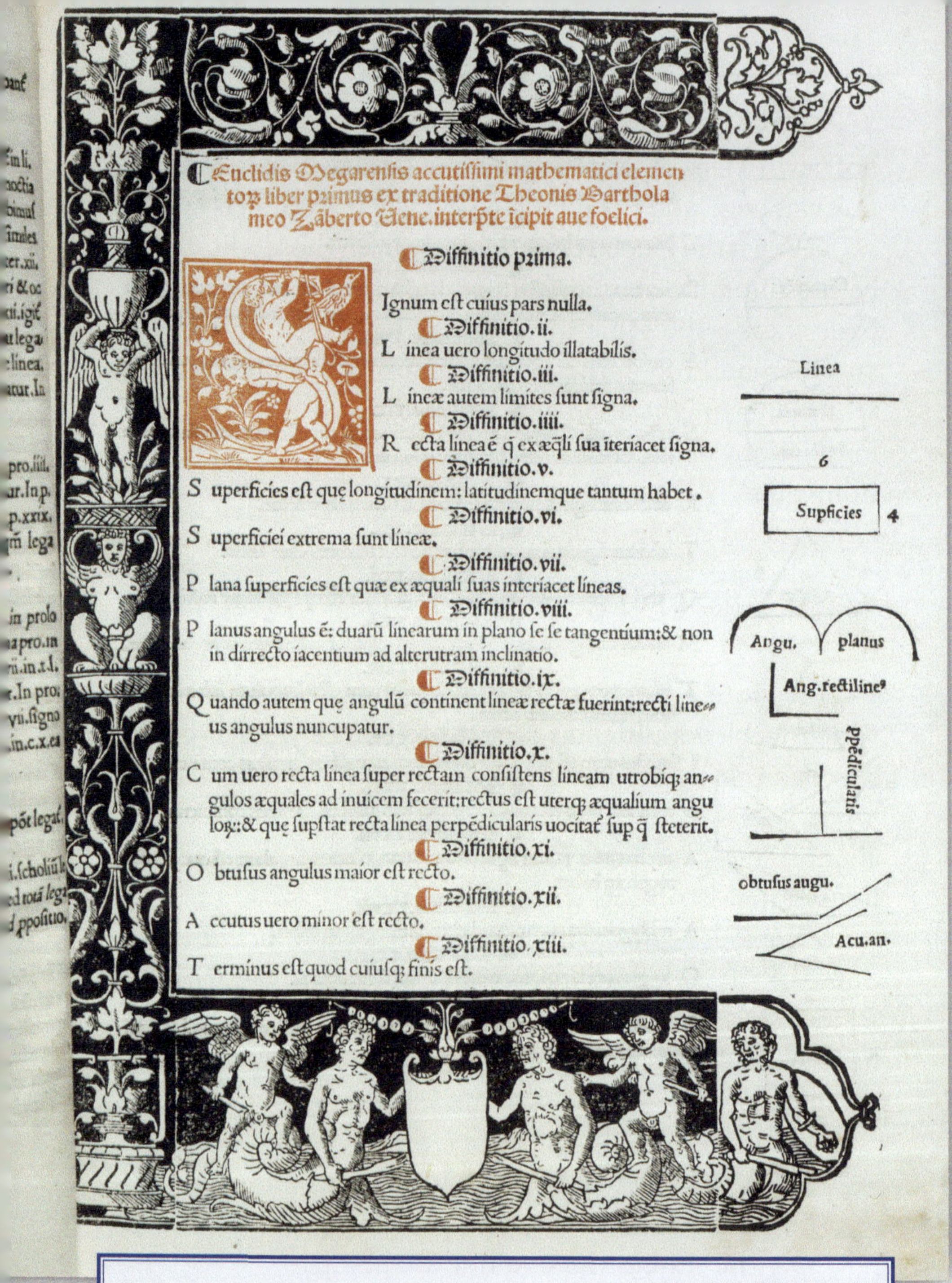

Euclidis Megarensis accutissimi mathematici elementoꝝ liber primus ex traditione Theonis Bartholameo Zaberto Uene. interpte icipit aue foelici.

Diffinitio prima.

Signum est cuius pars nulla.

Diffinitio. ii.

Linea uero longitudo illatabilis.

Diffinitio. iii.

Lineæ autem limites sunt signa.

Diffinitio. iiii.

Recta linea ē q̄ ex æq̄li sua iteriacet signa.

Diffinitio. v.

Superficies est quę longitudinem: latitudinemque tantum habet.

Diffinitio. vi.

Superficiei extrema sunt lineæ.

Diffinitio. vii.

Plana superficies est quæ ex æquali suas interiacet lineas.

Diffinitio. viii.

Planus angulus ē: duarū linearum in plano se se tangentium: & non in directo iacentium ad alterutram inclinatio.

Diffinitio. ix.

Quando autem quę angulū continent lineæ rectæ fuerint: recti lineus angulus nuncupatur.

Diffinitio. x.

Cum uero recta linea super rectam consistens lineam utrobiq; angulos æquales ad inuicem fecerit: rectus est uterq; æqualium angulorum: & quę supstat recta linea perpēdicularis uocitat̄ sup q̄ steterit.

Diffinitio. xi.

Obtusus angulus maior est recto.

Diffinitio. xii.

Accutus uero minor est recto.

Diffinitio. xiii.

Terminus est quod cuiusq; finis est.

This page of definitions from Elements *Book I is from a 1510 Latin translation by Bartolommeo Zamberti. It has a decorative border with playful cupids.*

5. A surface is that which has length and breadth only.

There are a total of twenty-three definitions in the first book. Here are a few more:

6. An obtuse angle is an angle greater than a right angle.
7. A circle is a plane figure contained by one line such that all the straight lines falling upon it from one point among those lying within the figure are equal to one another.
8. And the point is called the center of the circle.

The last definition in the book deals with what is meant by "parallel."

9. Parallel straight lines are straight lines which, being in the same plane and being produced indefinitely in both directions, do not meet one another in either direction.

Following the definitions, Book I lists five "postulates." The postulates use the same words Euclid defined in his twenty-three definitions. That way there's no question as to what is meant. If the reader is confused, all he has to do is refer back to the definitions for guidance. The first three postulates covered the ways in which a person can construct a geometric figure. As Euclid wrote, one can do so:

1. by drawing a straight line from any point to any point
2. by producing a finite straight line continuously in a straight line
3. by describing a circle with any center and distance

The last two postulates in Book I are as follows:

4. All right angles are equal to one another.
5. If a straight line falling on two straight lines make the interior angles on the same side less than two right angles, the two straight lines, if produced indefinitely, meet on that side on which are the angles less than the two right angles.

Euclid followed up his postulates with a list of "common notions." The common notions are what today we would call axioms. An axiom is a self-evident truth. It's obviously true to anyone who reads it.

Euclid includes five common notions in Book I. All five are about equality.

1. Things which are equal to the same thing are also equal to one another.
2. If equals be added to equals, the wholes are equal.
3. If equals be subtracted from equals, the remainders are equal.
4. Things which coincide with one another are equal to one another.
5. The whole is greater than the part.

You might notice something about Euclid's style. He's very orderly. Everything comes in a neat package, clearly presented for easy reading. He uses logic. He doesn't jump from one idea to another completely unrelated idea. Instead, he uses each idea to build, logically, to the next one.

The rest of *Elements* is full of more definitions, problems, diagrams, and enough challenging geometry to keep any student of the subject busy for years. Book II, for example, delves into the geometry of rectangles. Book III is about circles, and Book IV deals with constructions of polygons in circles. Book V discusses a general theory of proportion that originates from Eudoxus. Book VI explains the properties of similarity for rectilinear figures. Books VII through IX describe the theory of whole numbers. Book X involves a theory of irrational lines and is rooted in the contributions of Theaetetus and Eudoxus. Book XI sets out definitions concerning solid geometry. Book XII focuses on pyramids, cones, and cylinders and covers areas and volumes. Book XIII discusses the five regular solids, called the Platonic solids, and describes how to inscribe or construct them in a given sphere.

Historians of mathematics will never know for sure which parts of *Elements* came entirely from Euclid and which relied in whole or in part on the work of earlier geometers and mathematicians. All agree, however, that that's not the point. The genius of *Elements*, they'll tell you, is not in where the information came from. It's how that information is presented and how that presentation changed geometry forever.

EUCLID'S MOST ILLUSTRIOUS POSTULATE

Euclid's most famous postulate is his fifth. It's the postulate he later uses as the foundation for a discussion on parallel lines. Here it is again: "If a straight line falling on

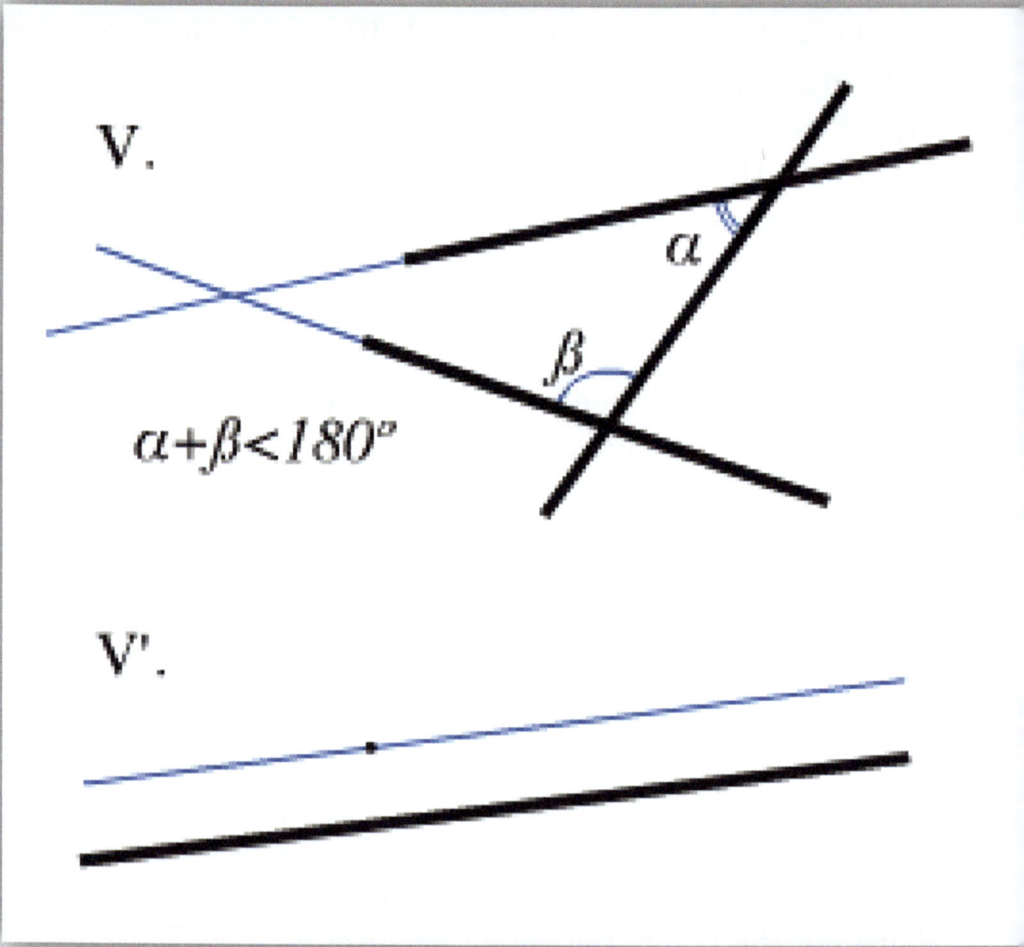

This figure represents Euclid's acclaimed fifth postulate: If a straight line falling on two straight lines make the interior angles on the same side less than two right angles, the two straight lines, if produced indefinitely, meet on that side on which are the angles less than the two right angles.

two straight lines make the interior angles on the same side less than two right angles, the two straight lines, if produced indefinitely, meet on that side on which are the angles less than the two right angles.

Why is this postulate so well known? For one, it's long and complicated—far more so than any of the others. That's not what attracts mathematicians, though. Ever since Euclid wrote it, math experts have called it inadequate because there is no way to prove it is true. Euclid himself had questions about the fifth postulate. He tried to find a way to prove its truth but could not. In the end, he decided it was impossible to do so.

This, of course, presented Euclid with a problem. Because he couldn't prove the postulate true, how would he continue on with his book, in which everything written depended on everything before it? If his foundation wasn't solid, how would he build? Euclid's solution was simple. He just assumed the fifth postulate was true, and he moved on.

Although this may have satisfied Euclid, it didn't make the skeptics happy. For hundreds of years, mathematicians around the world did everything they could to prove the fifth postulate. But no one succeeded.

Some geometers instead offered provable alternatives to the fifth postulate that they believed could be used in its place. One of the most acclaimed of these alternatives was what is today called Playfair's axiom after John Playfair, a Scottish mathematician who lived in the late eighteenth and early nineteenth centuries. "Through a given point in a plane, one and only one line can be drawn parallel to a

SOME TEXTS ATTRIBUTED TO EUCLID

Some historians believe Euclid wrote other books that have since disappeared. To back up their claims, they cite the writings of other ancient philosophers and mathematicians who sometimes refer to a Euclid in their works and give Euclid credit for certain texts. But these texts are lost forever, so it's impossible to know for sure if Euclid truly did have a part in their creation.

One book, *Catoptrica*, is still in print today, although it's likely very different from the original version. It discusses reflection and uses geometry to explain it. While some experts doubt Euclid had anything to do with this book, others believe at least a portion of the material is derived from his work.

Other books that some believe are Euclid's cannot be found anywhere. In *Pseudaria*—a book that Proclus, the early philosopher, called "The Book of Fallacies"—Euclid supposedly demonstrated how many of the ideas about geometry during and prior to his time were wrong. He apparently did so through use of his proven theorems, which time and time again showed that the old conclusions had to be in error.

Another text attributed to Euclid but nowhere to be found is *Surface-Loci*. Supposedly

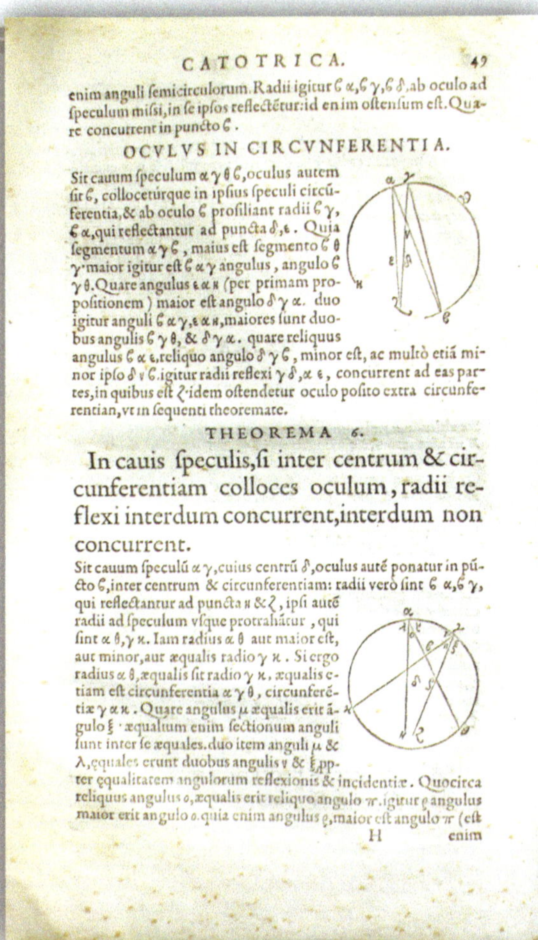

CATOTRICA. 49

enim anguli ſemicirculorum. Radii igitur ϐα, ϐγ, ϐδ, ab oculo ad ſpeculum miſſi, in ſe ipſos reflectétur: id enim oſtenſum eſt. Quare concurrent in puncto ϐ.

OCVLVS IN CIRCVNFERENTIA.

Sit cauum ſpeculum αγθϐ, oculus autem ſit ϐ, collocetúrque in ipſius ſpeculi circũferentia, & ab oculo ϐ proſiliant radii ϐγ, ϐα, qui reflectantur ad puncta δ, ε. Quia ſegmentum αγϐ, maius eſt ſegmento ϐθγ: maior igitur eſt ϐαγ angulus, angulo ϐγθ. Quare angulus εακ (per primam propoſitionem) maior eſt angulo δγα. duo igitur anguli ϐαγ, εακ, maiores ſunt duobus angulis ϐγθ, & δγα. quare reliquus angulus ϐαε, reliquo angulo δγϐ, minor eſt, ac multò etiã minor ipſo δνϐ. igitur radii reflexi γδ, αε, concurrent ad eas partes, in quibus eſt ζ: idem oſtendetur oculo poſito extra circunferentian, vt in ſequenti theoremate.

THEOREMA 6.

In cauis ſpeculis, ſi inter centrum & circunferentiam colloces oculum, radii reflexi interdum concurrent, interdum non concurrent.

Sit cauum ſpeculũ αγ, cuius centrũ δ, oculus autẽ ponatur in pũcto ϐ, inter centrum & circunferentiam: radii verò ſint ϐα, ϐγ, qui reflectantur ad puncta κ & ζ, ipſi autẽ radii ad ſpeculum vſque protrahãtur, qui ſint αθ, γκ. Iam radius αθ aut maior eſt, aut minor, aut æqualis radio γκ. Si ergo radius αθ, æqualis ſit radio γκ, æqualis etiam eſt circunferentia αγθ, circunferẽtiæ γακ. Quare angulus μ æqualis erit ãgulo ξ: æqualium enim ſectionum anguli ſunt inter ſe æquales. duo item anguli μ & λ, ęquales erunt duobus angulis ν & ξ, ppter ęqualitatem angulorum reflexionis & incidentiæ. Quocirca reliquus angulus ο, æqualis erit reliquo angulo π. igitur ρ angulus maior erit angulo ο. quia enim angulus ρ, maior eſt angulo π (eſt

H enim

This page is from a Latin edition of Catoptrica, *a book that was printed in 1604. It was a work about mirrors and the reflection of light, and Proclus attributed the original text to Euclid.*

written in two separate books, *Surface-Loci* is said to have discussed the geometrical relationships between points found on surfaces.

Still another book, *Porisms*, is believed to have delved deeply into complicated geometry. Some experts think this book would have shown Euclid to have been a far more advanced mathematician than he is given credit for being.

Three other books that some attribute to Euclid but that most disregard completely when

(continued on the next page)

(continued from previous page)

discussing his work are *The Elements of Music, Sectio Canonis,* and *Introduction to Harmony.* All three are about sound. In addition, some have said Euclid may have authored several texts about mechanics, the science and physics behind movement. In all these cases, however, there is no conclusive evidence to prove Euclid is the author. Although each book may contain details that are suspiciously similar to Euclid's known works, none is definitively his. This very fact—that so many books without known authors are commonly attributed to Euclid—attests to Euclid's lasting influence. Even in death, thousands of years after he thought and wrote and lived, his ideas survive in the works of others.

given line." Playfair's axiom is well known today among beginning geometry students because it's relatively easy to understand. Of course, just because something is easy doesn't mean it's any better, and most experts agreed that Playfair's was not good enough to replace the fifth postulate. So the fifth postulate remained, forever a part of Euclid's *Elements*.

EUCLID'S *DATA, DIVISION OF FIGURES, PHAENOMENA,* AND *OPTICS*

Although *Elements* was by far Euclid's most renowned and respected work, it was by no means all he had to offer the world. In fact, for his time Euclid was quite a productive author. He is believed to have written many different books, some of which have survived through the ages and others that have apparently disappeared forever. All the books today that are attributed to Euclid are on mathematics. All have been essentially ignored because of their relative lack of importance when compared to *Elements*. For those who wish to understand just who Euclid was, however, these books play an important role. Unlike *Elements*, which for the most part compiled and organized the material of Euclid's predecessors, these other books—including *Data*, *On Divisions of Figures*, *Phaenomena*, and *Optics*—cover his personal work in mathematics.

Data discusses geometrical proofs in plane geometry. In a proof—an essential part of geometry and all mathematics—the mathematician uses logic and reason to establish the truth of a statement. Many scholars view *Data* as being closely aligned to the first four books of Euclid's *Elements*. *On Divisions of Figures* covers the division of geometric figures into smaller parts. *Phaenomena* delves into how geometry can be used in astronomy. *Optics* deals with the geometry of vision and perspectives. For example, how from very far away something that is big can look small to the human eye.

Sculptor Nino Pisano made this marble relief of Euclid holding a compass in the fourteenth century. Euclid's Elements *became the standard text on geometry and many scholars believe it has been published more times than any book besides the Bible.*

These books all show that Euclid was, first and foremost, a mathematician. He must have been fascinated by shapes, numbers, and ratios and must have wondered how they applied to everyday life. As one of the leading thinkers in a time of great progress and excitement, Euclid must have spent countless hours pondering the significance of his work. Perhaps he realized that one day his thoughts on mathematics would lead to something big.

CHAPTER FIVE

The Significance of Euclid and His Work

A product of the life and times that surrounded him in 300 BCE, Euclid had incredible intellectual vision. He turned to the works of his predecessors to launch his own career pursuing a subject that both fascinated and challenged him. During his life, Euclid was well respected by his peers. For the most part, his fellow citizens—including Greek philosophers, mathematicians, and scientists—looked up to him. They saw him as an innovator, as a man who was unafraid to take big new steps in his field and risk the criticisms of those who might disagree. He was everything one might expect in an intellectual leader of ancient Greece.

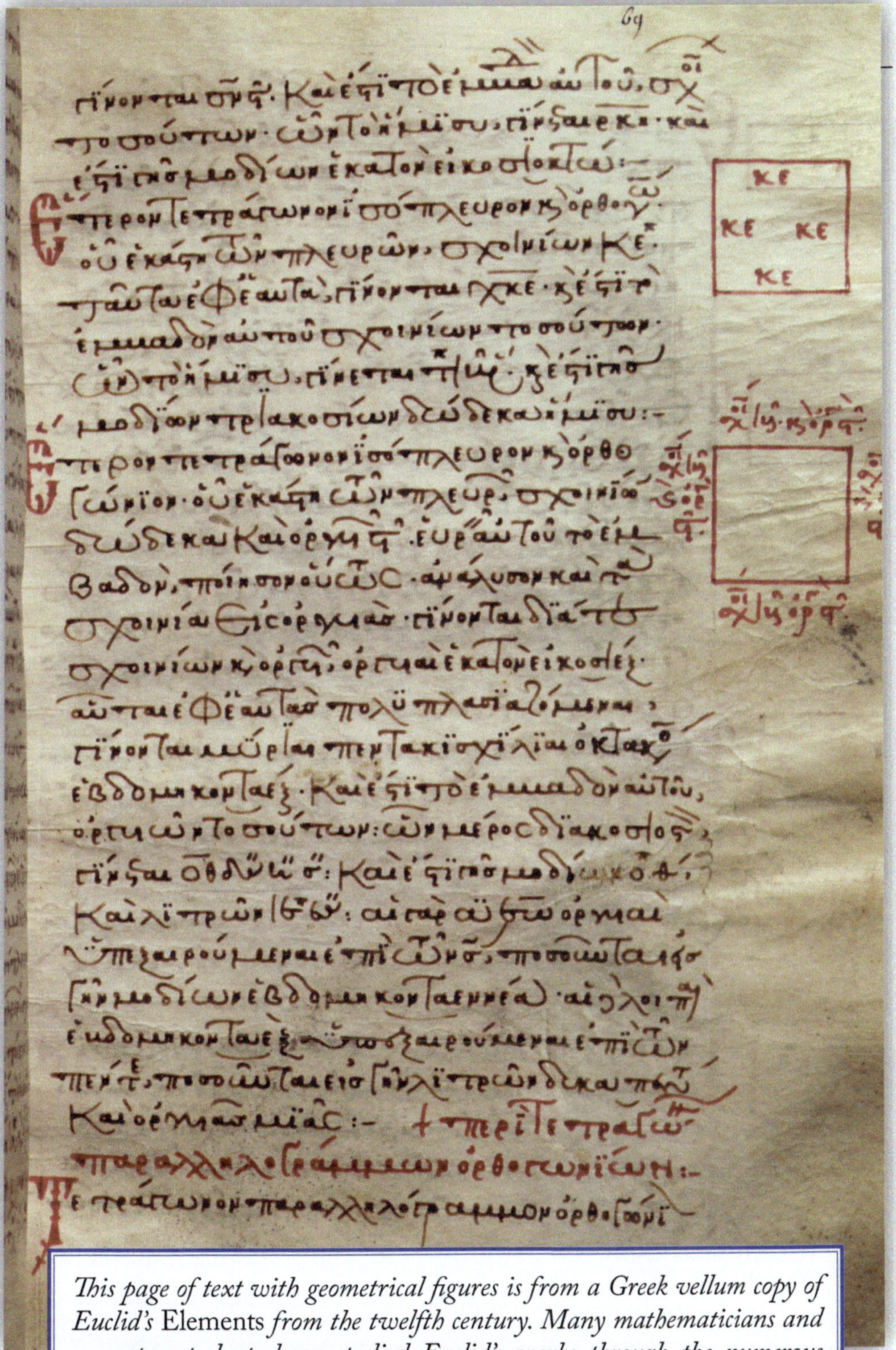

This page of text with geometrical figures is from a Greek vellum copy of Euclid's Elements *from the twelfth century. Many mathematicians and geometry students have studied Euclid's works through the numerous translations throughout the centuries.*

People who did find fault in Euclid's work were probably unhappy with his unwavering attention to every last detail. They questioned why this man saw it necessary to include the simplest of mathematical proofs to prove something that to them seemed so completely obvious. Perhaps they believed there were more important things to do than break geometry down to its elements, as Euclid had done. They didn't see the genius in Euclid's move toward the basics.

Upon Euclid's death, not much changed. Or at least not right away. He still had both critics and enthusiasts. Eventually, though, his fame and reputation grew as *Elements* became known as the best book available for beginning mathematics students. *Elements* was required reading for any aspiring mathematician. In a region where education and learning were valued in the same way as the democratic freedoms of speech and debate, Euclid's book was critically important. It was a symbol of progress and perhaps of a future where mathematics would play an even greater role in the workings of the world.

Over time, as might be expected, people forgot about Euclid the person. But even as his life faded from memory, his greatest work lived on. Many commentaries were written on *Elements*. Designed to help guide students in their reading, these commentaries, most of which are now lost, sometimes found mistakes in Euclid's work, but more often than not wound up praising the author for his immeasurable contributions to mathematics. The fact that *Elements* was acknowledged to be the sole authority

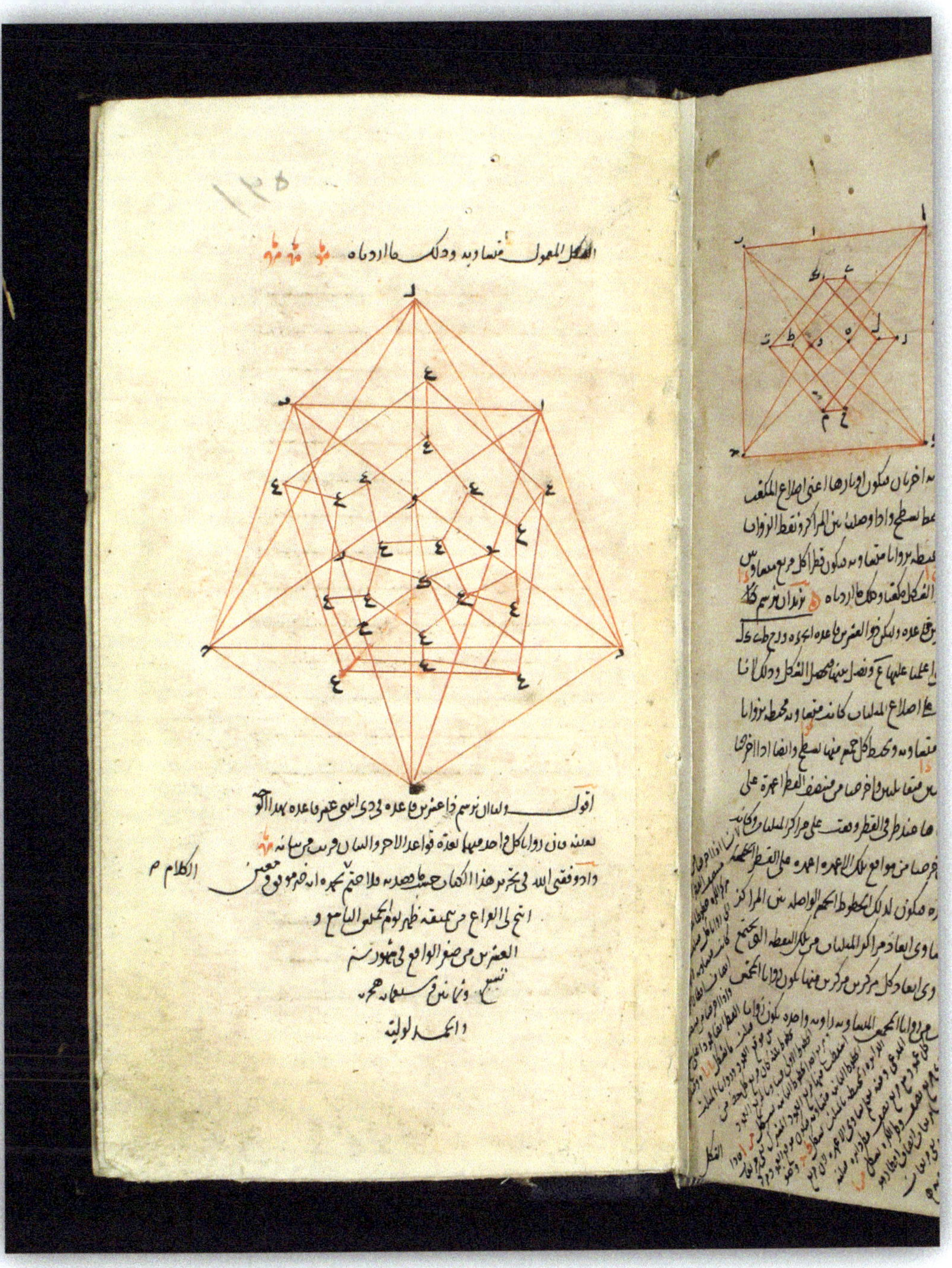

Nasr al-Din al-Tusi, a Persian scholar, wrote a commentary on Euclid's The Elements *in the thirteenth century. This version of his manuscript written in Arabic is from the fourteenth century.*

on the subject of geometry for so many centuries is a testament to Euclid's legacy that few mathematicians have matched.

Over hundreds of years, handwritten copies of *Elements* were distributed around the world. These copies came in many different translations and were read by thousands of eager young students. The first printed edition of *Elements* was finally published in 1482, nearly 1,800 years after Euclid wrote the book and just ten years before Christopher Columbus sailed to the Americas from Spain. It took almost another century for the first English edition of the book to appear in 1570. Since then, many more editions have been printed. Some of these editions have been edited and shortened, tailored to modern-day readers. Other editions have attempted to remain as close as possible to the original manuscript as written by Euclid.

ADAPTATIONS OF EUCLID'S *ELEMENTS*

It is believed that prior to the 1800s, most copies of *Elements* in circulation around the world were in fact based not on Euclid's original text but on an adaptation of it by another ancient Greek. Sometime in the late 300s, more than 600 years after Euclid's death, a mathematician named Theon of Alexandria decided he would edit the book to make it easier to read and to fix some errors that he found. He made many changes to the original and even incorporated the works of other authors into the text.

Project Euclid

A not-for-profit online publishing service called Project Euclid was developed by the Cornell University Library in Ithaca, New York, and is directed by Cornell University and Duke University Press in Durham, North Carolina. Project Euclid offers access to journals, monographs, and conference proceedings in the fields of theoretical mathematics and statistics. It provides a platform for small publishers of scholarly journals to transition from print to electronic publishing by collaborating with others to cut costs while advancing mathematical studies and communication. First launched by Cornell in 2003 with nineteen journals, Project Euclid now provides open access to more than sixty. In 2011, it received the Physics-Astronomy-Mathematics Division Award from the Special Libraries Association, in recognition of its contributions to the literature of physics, mathematics, or astronomy.

When he was finished, his version of *Elements* was, in many ways, quite different from Euclid's. Unfortunately, those who lived after Theon used *his* copy of *Elements*, and not Euclid's (which by then would have been extremely hard to find) to produce further editions. It wasn't until 1818 that an edition was produced that is believed to be much closer to Euclid's original.

EUCLID'S LEGACY

Today, Euclid's legacy continues, as high school geometry students are regularly taught the basics of the subject through passages from *Elements.* Geometry textbooks often quote Euclid's work and commonly use his examples and proofs to illustrate important points. Indeed, were it not for Euclid, proofs themselves may have never have become the standard in mathematics as they are today.

An artist's rendering of the European Space Agency's satellite Euclid *is shown here. A NASA team at the Jet Propulsion Laboratory in Pasadena, California, has been chosen to help in the mission that will study the mysteries of dark energy and dark matter in 2020.*

Geometry, and mathematics in general, has changed a lot since Euclid's day, but much also remains the same. People today turn to *Elements* to learn about the foundations of mathematics—to see where it all began and to learn the subject from the ground up. After all, there's no point in trying to understand Einstein's theory of relativity, or any of the other highly advanced mathematical concepts of today, if you don't have a solid grasp of the fundamentals. In 1783, the great German philosopher Immanuel Kant wrote, "There is no book at all in metaphysics such as we have in mathematics. If you want to know what mathematics is, just look at Euclid's *Elements*," according to *Euclid: The Creation of Mathematics*.

Even the European Space Agency (ESA) honored the great geometer by calling its space mission to map the geometry of the dark universe after Euclid. According to the ESA's website, this mission "will investigate the distance-redshift relationship and the evolution of cosmic structures by measuring shapes and redshifts of galaxies and clusters of galaxies out to...10 billion years." The launch of the *Euclid* satellite is expected to take place in 2020. It will be equipped with a silicon carbide mirror telescope and instruments that will probe the history and physics of the universe. In January 2013, the National Aeronautics and Space Administration (NASA) announced that it had joined the ESA's Euclid mission by planning to contribute a near-infrared spectrometer and imaging photometer to the mission.

Abraham Lincoln and Stephen A. Douglas are depicted during their political debates in Illinois in 1858. Lincoln stated that he used Euclid's approach in logic and geometry in facets of his life and work.

Euclid's life may be a mystery, but his legacy is well known. The great mathematicians who followed Euclid—from Archimedes to Galileo (who allegedly listened to lectures on Euclid at the University of Pisa) to Sir Isaac Newton—all studied his work. According to Drew R. McCoy's article "An 'Old-Fashioned' Nationalism: Lincoln, Jefferson, and the Classical Tradition," a fellow lawyer stated that Abraham Lincoln carried a copy of *The Elements* when he was a traveling lawyer, and it became apparent later that he mastered the first six books of Euclid's work. Lincoln was said to be enamored of the logical approach of Euclid's work and applied this approach to aspects of his life and even in his speeches. In a political speech in Columbus, Ohio, in 1859, Lincoln said:

> There are two ways of establishing a proposition. One is by trying to demonstrate it upon reason, and the other is, to show that great men in former times have thought so and so, and thus to pass it by the weight of pure authority. Now, if Judge Douglas [Stephen A. Douglas] will demonstrate somehow that this is popular sovereignty,—the right of one man to make a slave of another, without any right in that other, or anyone else to object,—demonstrate it as Euclid demonstrated propositions,—there is no objection. But when he comes forward, seeking to carry a principle by bringing it to the authority of men who themselves utterly repudiate that principle, I ask that he shall not be permitted to do it.

All these people, not surprisingly, were profoundly influenced by *Elements*, as traces of Euclid's ideas and methods are evident in their own contributions to math, science, and speech making. The fact is, the world as people know it now—even though it's very different from and far more complicated than it was more than two thousand years ago—wouldn't be the same without Euclid. This man, the founding father of geometry, could not have known what his work would do for those who followed him. But if he had, he certainly would have been pleased.

TIMELINE

CIRCA 1200 BCE The Mycenaean civilization ends and ancient Greek civilization begins.

776 BCE The first Olympic Games are held, according to historical records.

CIRCA 624 BCE Thales of Miletus is born.

CIRCA 600 BCE The dawn of Greek democracy.

CIRCA 570 BCE Pythagoras of Samos is born.

CIRCA 547 BCE Thales dies.

492 BCE The Persian Wars begin.

CIRCA 490 BCE Pythagoras dies.

CIRCA 480 BCE The beginning of the Classical Age of Greece.

CIRCA 470 BCE Socrates is born.

449 BCE The Persian Wars end.

CIRCA 428 BCE Plato is born.

CIRCA 417 BCE The mathematician Theaetetus is born in Athens.

CIRCA 395 BCE Eudoxus of Cnidus is born.

CIRCA 384 BCE Aristotle is born.

CIRCA 369 BCE Theaetetus dies in Athens.

CIRCA 356 BCE Alexander the Great is born.

CIRCA 342 BCE Eudoxus dies.

336 BCE Philip II is assassinated, and his son, Alexander, becomes king of Macedon.

331 BCE Alexander founds the city of Alexandria in Egypt.

CIRCA 300 BCE Euclid flourishes.

323 BCE Alexander the Great dies, marking the end of the ancient Greek period and Classical Age and the beginning of the Hellenistic Age.

322 BCE Aristotle dies.

304 BCE Ptolemy I becomes king of Egypt.

CIRCA 300 BCE Euclid completes *Elements*.

282 BCE Ptolemy I dies.

CIRCA 287 BCE Archimedes is born.

CIRCA 265 BCE Euclid dies.

146 BCE Greece is integrated into the Roman Empire, marking the end of the Hellenistic Age.

31 BCE The Hellenistic Period ends when Rome conquers its last Hellenistic kingdom in Egypt.

193–211 CE Septimius Severus is Roman emperor.

CIRCA 410 CE Proclus is born.

1482 The first printed edition in Latin of *Elements* appears.

1570 The first English edition of *Elements* appears.

1594 The first Arabic version of Euclid's *Elements* is printed.

1642 Isaac Newton is born.

1840S Abraham Lincoln reads *Elements* and masters Euclid's propositions.

2003 Project Euclid is established at Cornell University Library in Ithaca, New York.

2020 The European Space Agency will launch the satellite *Euclid* to map the geometry of the dark universe.

GLOSSARY

AXIOM A postulate, an accepted statement of fact; for example, all right angles are equal to one another.

CLASSICAL AGE A period (490–323 BCE) in ancient Greece characterized by progress in art, architecture, science, democracy, and other ideals of the time.

COMMENTARY A written interpretation, explanation, or critique of someone else's work.

CONCENTRIC Shapes, such as circles or arcs, that share the same center, the larger shape often completely surrounding the smaller ones.

DEMOCRACY A system of government in which people are granted a voice in civic and political affairs.

GEOMETRY A branch of mathematics that deals with the measurement, properties, and relationships of points, lines, shapes, angles, surfaces, and solids.

INSCRIBE In geometry, to draw a figure within another so that their boundaries touch but do not cross.

LUMINARY A person who influences, inspires, or has achieved success in his or her chosen field.

MATHEMATICS The science of numbers and their relationships.

MECHANICS The branch of mathematics that involves motion and the forces producing motion.

ORACLE In ancient Greece, a priest or priestess through whom a god is supposed to speak and give advice; a shrine in which a god reveals advice or prophesies.

PAPYRUS A type of paper made from a tall, woody reed plant.

PARALLEL Two lines that extend in the same direction but do not meet.

PHILOSOPHER One who seeks wisdom.

POSTULATE A claim that is put forth and accepted as true.

PREDECESSOR One who comes before.

PROOF A method used in mathematics to establish the truth of a mathematical statement.

PROPOSITION A statement or claim that expresses a concept that can be true or false; in math, a formal statement of a problem or theorem.

SCROLL A roll of material on which documents may be written.

SKEPTIC A person who doubts whether something is true.

THEOREM A proposition or statement in mathematics shown to be true through the logical use of other previously established truths or accepted axioms.

For More Information

American Mathematical Society (AMS)
21 Charles Street
Providence, RI 02904
(401) 455-4100
Website: http://www.ams.org

The AMS offers programs for students in the mathematical sciences, including a summer math camp; online materials for math help; a list of local math clubs; an online magazine, *Plus,* which features math-related articles and puzzles; and math competitions.

Association for Women in Mathematics (AWM)
11240 Waples Mill Road, Suite 200
Fairfax, VA 22030
(703) 934-0163
Website: http://www.awm-math.org

The AWM's mission is to encourage women and girls to study math and to pursue careers in the mathematical sciences.

MATHCOUNTS Foundation
1420 King Street

Alexandria, VA 22314

(703) 299-9006

Website: http://mathcounts.org

The MATHCOUNTS Foundation is a nonprofit organization that provides math competitions, information about math clubs, and Math Video Challenge, which helps students in making their own videos to teach math.

Mathematical Staircase, Inc.

278 Bay Road

Hadley, MA 01035

Website: http://www.mathstaircase.org

This organization provides educational programs to assist high school and college students in learning math and applying it to their daily lives. It also offers a summer program called MathILy, which helps students improve problem-solving skills and explore math in creative ways.

The Math League

Website: http://www.themathleague.com

This organization offers math contests to students (grades four to twelve) to encourage participation in math activities and to help them gain recognition for their accomplishments in math.

The National Museum of Mathematics
11 East 26th Street
New York, NY 10010
(212) 542-0566
Website: http://momath.org
This museum encourages the study of mathematics and displays exhibits involving the wonders of math.

Thomas Fisher Rare Book Library
University of Toronto
120 St. George Street
Toronto, ON M5S 1A5
Canada
(416) 978-5285
Website: http://fisher.library.utoronto.ca
This library contains numerous works of Renaissance scientists and early editions of Greek mathematicians, including Diophantus of Alexandria, Archimedes, Pappus of Alexandria,

Apollonius of Perga, and Euclid. It also includes a first Latin edition of Euclid's *The Elements*, printed by Ratdolt at Venice in 1482, the Greek edition (Basel, 1533), and the first printed Arabic version (Rome, 1594), among early translations in Italian, English, and German.

WEBSITES

Because of the changing nature of Internet links, Rosen Publishing has developed an online list of websites related to the subject of this book. This site is updated regularly. Please use this link to access the list:

http://www.rosenlinks.com/GGP/Euc

For further Reading

Artmann, Benno. *Euclid: The Creation of Mathematics.* New York, NY: Springer, 2013.

Bardi, Jason Socrates. *The Fifth Postulate: How Unraveling a Two-Thousand-Year-Old Mystery Unraveled the Universe.* Hoboken, NJ: John Wiley & Sons, Inc., 2009.

Bellos, Alex. *Here's Looking at Euclid: A Surprising Excursion Through the Astonishing World of Math.* New York, NY: Free Press, 2010.

Benham, Fred. *A Brief History of Math and Science. Book 4—Euclid, Archimedes, and the Astronomers* (Pyramids, Plato, and Planets). CreateSpace, 2012.

Berlinski, David. *The King of Infinite Space: Euclid and His Elements.* New York, NY: Basic Books, 2013.

Byrne, Oliver. *The First Six Books of Elements of Euclid.* Cologne, Germany: Taschen, 2013.

Gregersen, Erik, ed. *The Britannica Guide to the History of Mathematics* (Math Explained). New York, NY: Britannica Educational Publishing and Rosen Educational Services, 2011.

Heath, Sir Thomas. *A History of Greek Mathematics. Volume 1 From Thales to Euclid.* Mineola, NY: Dover Publications, 1981.

Heath, Sir Thomas. *A Manual of Greek Mathematics.* Mineola, NY: Dover Publications, 2003.

Heath, Sir Thomas, and Dana Densmore. *Euclid's Elements: All Thirteen Books Complete in One Volume.* Santa Fe, NM: Green Lion Press, 2013.

Hightower, Paul. *The Father of Geometry: Euclid and His 3-D World* (Great Minds of Ancient Science and Math). Berkeley Heights, NJ: Enslow Publishers, 2010.

Hodgkin, Luke Howard. *A History of Mathematics: From Mesopotamia to Modernity.* Oxford, England: Oxford University Press, 2013.

Hosch, William L., ed. *The Britannica Guide to Geometry* (Math Explained). New York, NY: Britannica Educational Publishing and Rosen Educational Services, 2011.

Pickover, Clifford A. *Archimedes to Hawking: Laws of Science and the Great Minds Behind Them.* New York, NY: Oxford University Press, 2008.

Stankowski, James, ed. *Geometry and Trigonometry* (The Story of Math: Core Principles of Mathematics). New York, NY: Britannica Educational Publishing and Rosen Educational Services, 2015.

Bibliography

Artmann, Benno. *Euclid: The Creation of Mathematics*. New York, NY: Springer, 1999.

Berggren, J. L., and R. S. D. Thomas. *Euclid's Phaenomena: A Translation and Study of a Hellenistic Treatise in Spherical Astronomy*. New York, NY: Garland Publishing Inc., 1996.

Berlinski, David. *The King of Infinite Space: Euclid and His Elements*. New York, NY: Basic Books, 2013.

Boyer, Carl B. *A History of Mathematics*. New York, NY: John Wiley & Sons, Inc., 1968.

Christides, Giorgos. "Greeks Captivated by Alexander-era Tomb at Amphipolis." *BBC News*.com. September 22, 2014. Retrieved November 21, 2014 (http://www.bbc.com/news/world-europe-29239529).

Craig, Edward, ed. "Geometry, Philosophical Issues In." *Routledge Encyclopedia of Philosophy, Vol. 4*. London, England: Routledge, 1998.

Cuomo, S. *Ancient Mathematics*. London, England: Routledge, 2001.

ESA Science & Technology. "Euclid." Retrieved December 8, 2014 (http://sci.esa.int/euclid).

Euclid. *The Thirteen Books of Euclid's Elements.* New York, NY: Dover Publications, Inc., 1956.

Ganchy, Sally. *Islam and Science, Medicine, and Technology* (Understanding Islam). New York, NY: Rosen Publishing, 2009.

Greenberg, Marvin Jay. *Euclidean and Non-Euclidean Geometries: Development and History.* 4th ed. New York, NY: W. H. Freeman and Company, 2008.

Gutierrez, Antonio. "Math Quotes." Abraham Lincoln. Retrieved December 9, 2014 (http://www.gogeometry.com/math_geometry_quotes/lincoln_abraham_geometry_euclid.html).

Hall, Edith. *Introducing the Ancient Greeks: From Bronze Age Seafarers to Navigators of the Western Mind.* New York, NY: W. W. Norton & Company, 2014.

Heath, Sir Thomas. *A History of Greek Mathematics, Vol. 1, From Thales to Euclid.* New York, NY: Dover Publications, Inc., 1981.

History.com. "Classical Greece." Retrieved November 21, 2014 (http://www.history.com/topics/ancient-history/classical-greece).

Hollar, Sherman, ed. *Ancient Egypt* (Ancient Civilizations). New York, NY: Britannica

Educational Publishing and Rosen Educational Services, 2012.

Hornblower, Simon, and Antony Spawforth, eds. *The Oxford Companion to Classical Civilization.* New York, NY: Oxford University Press, 1998.

Hosch, William L., ed. *The Britannica Guide to Algebra and Trigonometry* (Math Explained). New York, NY: Britannica Educational Publishing and Rosen Educational Services, 2011.

Hosch, William L., ed. *The Britannica Guide to Geometry* (Math Explained). New York, NY: Britannica Educational Publishing and Rosen Educational Services, 2011.

Kuiper, Kathleen, ed. *Ancient Greece: From the Archaic Period to the Death of Alexander the Great* (The Britannica Guide to Ancient Civilizations). New York, NY: Britannica Educational Publishing and Rosen Educational Services, 2011.

Lawler, Andrew. "Raising Alexandria." *Smithsonian Magazine.* April 2007. Retrieved November 21, 2014 (http://www.smithsonianmag.com/science-nature/raising-alexandria-151005550/?page=1).

Lincoln, Abraham. *Political Debates Between Abraham Lincoln and Stephen A. Douglas.* Cleveland, OH: Burrows Bros. Co., 1897; Bartleby.com, 2001. Retrieved December 9, 2014 (http://www.bartleby.com/br/251.html).

Mastin, Luke. "Hellenistic Mathematics—Euclid." The Story of Mathematics. 2010. Retrieved November 14, 2014 (http://www.storyofmathematics.com/hellenistic_euclid.html).

McCoy, Drew R. "An 'Old-Fashioned' Nationalism: Lincoln, Jefferson, and the Classical Tradition." *Journal of the Abraham Lincoln Association.* Volume 23, Issue 1, Winter 2002, pp. 55–67. Retrieved December 9, 2014 (http://quod.lib.umich.edu/j/jala/2629860.0023.104/--old-fashioned-nationalism-lincoln-jefferson?rgn=main;view=fulltext#note_25).

NASA. "Euclid. Mapping the Geometry of the Dark Universe." Retrieved December 8, 2014 (http://www.nasa.gov/mission_pages/euclid/main/index.html#.VIYfg4eyNNk).

Ostermann, Alexander, and Gerhard Wanner. *Geometry by Its History* (Undergraduate Texts in

Mathematics: Reading in Mathematics). New York, NY: Springer-Verlag, 2012.

Project Euclid. "Project Euclid: Mission and Goals." Retrieved December 8, 2014 (https://projecteuclid.org/about).

Speake, Graham, ed. "Euclid." *Encyclopedia of Greece and the Hellenic Tradition, Vol. 1.* London, England: Fitzroy Dearborn Publishers, 2000.

Special Libraries Association. "2011 PAM Division Award." June 23, 2011. Retrieved December 8, 2014 (http://pam.sla.org/2011/06/2011-pam-division-award).

Stankowski, James, ed. *Geometry and Trigonometry* (The Story of Math: Core Principles of Mathematics). New York, NY: Britannica Educational Publishing and Rosen Educational Services, 2015.

Terry, Leon. *The Mathmen.* New York, NY: McGraw-Hill, 1964.

UKessays. "The Life and Work of Euclid Philosophy Essay." Retrieved December 8, 2014 (http://www.ukessays.com/essays/philosophy/the-life-and-work-of-euclid-philosophy-essay.php).

University of St. Andrews, School of Mathematics and Statistics. "The Academy of Plato." August 2004. Retrieved December 9, 2014 (http://www-history.mcs.st-and.ac.uk/Societies/Plato.html).

Young, Robyn V., ed. "Euclid of Alexandria." *Notable Mathematicians: From Ancient Times to the Present.* Detroit, MI: Gale Research, 1998.

Index

ABOUT THE AUTHORS

Josette Campbell has studied algebra and axiomatic geometry for many years. She has been especially inspired by Euclid's postulates and frequently re-examines them carefully. Campbell resides in upstate New York.

Chris Hayhurst is a writer who lives in New Hampshire. His interest in both philosophy and mathematics can be traced to high school, where he first read Plato and discovered pi, and to college, where he was exposed to the teachings of Socrates and other great philosophers.

PHOTO CREDITS

Cover Science Source/Getty Images; pp. 1, 3, 6–7 (background) Madredus/Shutterstock.com; pp. 8–9, 27 DEA/G. Dagli Orti/De Agostini/Getty Images; pp. 12, 30, 45, 63, 80 © dra_schwartz/iStock/Getty Images; p. 13 Peter Hermes Furian/Shutterstock.com; pp. 14–15, 34 De Agostini Picture Library/Getty Images; pp. 18–19 Ancient Art and Architecture Collection Ltd./Bridgeman Images; p. 21 Scala/Art Resources, NY; pp. 22–23 Universal History Archive/Getty Images; pp. 30–31 Print Collector/Hulton Archive/Getty Images; pp. 37 Library of Congress Prints and Photographs Division; pp. 40–41 National Galleries of Scotland, Dist. RMN-Grand Palais/Art Resource, NY; pp. 42–43 thelefty/Shutterstock.com; p. 46 Hulton Archive/Getty Images; pp. 50–51 Godong/Universal Images Group/Getty Images; pp. 56–57 Vatican Library; pp. 60–61 Leemage/Universal Images Group/Getty Images; pp. 64, 66, 75 Images copyright History of Science Collections, University of Oklahoma Libraries; p. 68 Art Resource, NY; p. 78 DEA/A. Dagli Orti/De Agostini/Getty Images; p. 81 Bibliotheque Nationale, Paris, France/Archives Charmet/Bridgeman Images; p. 83 Kharbine-Tapabor/The Art Archive at Art Resource, NY; pp. 86–87 ESA/C. Carreau; p. 89 Private Collection/Peter Newark American Pictures/Bridgeman Images.

Designer: Brian Garvey; Editor: Kathy Kuhtz-Campbell